Praise for *Let's Get Published*

Kirsty is a highly-skilled self-publishing expert, and in *Let's Get Published* she covers every aspect of launching a book into the world, including writing, editing, design, marketing, and all the fiddly stuff such as ISBNs and legal deposit with the National Library. Self-publishing has come a long way in the last few years, and Kirsty has provided an excellent guide to what can be a complicated process for new authors.

Michael Hanrahan – Managing Director, Publish Central; Co-founder, Australian Business Book Awards

Let's Get Published is a must-read for anybody wanting to learn about the complex world of book publishing. In this helpful resource, Kirsty provides a roadmap for writers to get started on their publishing journey. If you are looking for practical advice about how to self-publish your manuscript, this is the book for you.

Russell Perry – Director, Australian Authors Marketplace

Having collaborated with Kirsty and the Brisbane Self Publishing Service team on my two series of YA books, I'm no stranger to self-publishing. Nevertheless, I was keen to read *Let's Get Published*. Not only did it consolidate what I've already learned on my author journey, I also found fresh inspiration and information for tackling my next project. Don't set sail on your self-publishing adventure without this gem of a book!

Sarah Fisher – author of Dragonscale and Wehrdragon YA series

Congratulations, Kirsty, on taking the exciting step of publishing your own book – *Let's Get Published: The Self-Publishing Playbook*. Your extensive knowledge and expertise in the self-publishing space shines through on every page. I'm sure that the information you've shared in this book will greatly assist any author who wants to get started on their self-publishing journey.

Simone Feiler – Owner, Brisbane Audiobook Production

After meeting Kirsty Ogden in an online business group, then listening and watching her share details about her craft, I soon realised she stood out from the crowd. Kirsty is a dedicated and grounded professional who has a gift with helping writers to self-publish their books, whilst also keeping things simple. No doubt her own book, *Let's Get Published*, will prove to be a valuable resource for many people.

Cathy Dimarchos – TEDx speaker and award-winning global business advisor

Let's Get Published is one of the best books I have read on self-publishing, primarily because it makes the reader think about what they want, rather than telling them everything the author thinks they should do! It leads you on a journey from why you should write, how to write, to the essential editing process and design and layout concerns of your book, concluding with the important step of marketing. A perfect introduction for emerging writers, as well as anyone seeking clarity within the publishing jungle today. Highly recommended.

Jim Higgins – President, Fellowship of Australian Writers (Qld)

KIRSTY OGDEN

LET'S GET PUBLISHED

THE SELF-PUBLISHING PLAYBOOK

Brisbane Self Publishing Service

Published in Australia in 2022 by Brisbane Self Publishing Service

Website: www.brisbaneselfpublishing.com.au

Email: kirsty@brisbaneselfpublishing.com.au

© Kirsty Ogden 2022

The moral right of the author has been asserted.

All rights reserved.

Except as permitted under the *Australian Copyright Act 1968* (for example, a fair dealing for the purposes of study, research, criticism or review), no part of this publication may be reproduced, stored in a retrieval system, communicated or transmitted in any form or by any means without prior written permission.

All inquiries should be made to the author.

ISBN 9780645540703 (paperback)
ISBN 9780645540710 (ebook)

 A catalogue record for this book is available from the National Library of Australia

Disclaimer

The author has made every effort to ensure the information within this book was correct at the time of publication. Due to the dynamic nature of the internet, some website addresses or links contained in this book may have since changed and no longer be valid. To the maximum extent permitted by law, the author and publisher disclaim all responsibility and liability to any person, arising directly or indirectly from any person taking or not taking action based on the information in this book.

*Reach high, for stars lie hidden in you.
Dream deep, for every dream precedes the goal.*

— *Rabindranath Tagore*

Contents

Preface xi

Introduction 1

PART ONE – So You Want To Be An Author?

Chapter 1 – Before putting words on the page 7
  What is your motivation for publishing a book? 8
  Identifying the 'why' of your book 11
  Will people be interested in what you have to say? 13
  What's in a name? Pros and cons of using a pseudonym 14

Chapter 2 – To write or not to write 17
  You're not alone: ghostwriting and writing coaching 18
  Establishing timelines for your writing project 20
  Some tips for navigating common writing pitfalls 22
  How to overcome writer's block 24
  Sharing is caring: writers' groups, retreats and workshops 26

Chapter 3 – How to write it right 29
  Pinpointing your book's core theme or message 30
  Characteristics of a successful fiction book 32
  Crafting the perfect non-fiction book title and subtitle 35
  General writing rules (and whether it's okay to break them) 37
  Author's voice, style and tone: what are they, and how do you identify yours? 40

LET'S GET PUBLISHED

PART TWO – Editing Basics For Flawless Content

Chapter 4 – Your foundational editing checklist 45
- Self-editing and working with beta readers 47
- Editing and proofreading: how do they differ? 50
- Structural editing: the big-picture perspective 51
- Copyediting: crossing your 'T's and dotting your 'I's 53
- Proofreading: checking it twice ... and then checking again! 54
- What's your style? Style guides to the rescue 55
- Collaborating with a professional editor 57

Chapter 5 – Essential publishing issues to consider 61
- Potential legal 'red flags' for authors 63
- Ethical and cultural dilemmas ... and how to deal with them 67
- We're all equal: using inclusive language 68
- Citing references in your book 70

Chapter 6 – Getting the structure right for your book 73
- Everything in its correct place: typical structural elements of a book 74
- Copyright/imprint page: signalling ownership of your creative content 76
- Acknowledgements and dedications: thanking the key people 77
- Foreword, preface and introduction: what's the difference? 77
- The final curtain: conclusion, appendices, glossary and index 78
- Entice your audience: back cover blurb and author bio 80

PART THREE – The Perfect Package For Your Narrative

Chapter 7 – Between the covers: your book's internal design 85
- The optimal medium for your message 86
- Major influences on book layout design 88
- Fundamental elements of internal page formatting 90
- Which typefaces work best? 92
- Resolution is key: the benefits of high-resolution images 94
- Respecting other creatives' IP 95

Contents

Chapter 8 – Judging a book by its cover   99
  Anatomy of a book cover   101
  Fitting in versus standing out   102
  A prudent investment: working with a professional designer   104
  Designers aren't mind-readers: developing an effective design brief   106

Chapter 9 – Book publishing admin: mundane but important!   109
  What is an ISBN and why do you need it for your book?   109
  The difference between an ISBN and a barcode   111
  It's official: the legal deposit process   112

PART FOUR – Putting Your Best Book Forward

Chapter 10 – Which format suits your book?   117
  Common book formats for indie authors   118
  Print is not dead! Book printing options explained   120
  A cheap and cheerful guide to ebooks   124
  Audiobooks: a convenient product for our busy lives   127

PART FIVE – Let's Make A Sale

Chapter 11 – Book marketing for novices   133
  DIY or outsourcing: which approach should you take?   135
  Connecting with your ideal readers   136
  Developing an effective marketing strategy for your book   139
  Book marketing ideas for indie authors   140

Chapter 12 – Positioning yourself and your book for success   149
  You're a published author! What's next?   149
  Celebrate your success   151
  Building on lessons learned and planning your next book   152

Conclusion   155

Next steps   157

References and resources   159

Acknowledgements 167
About the author 169

Preface

As a writer, have you ever considered the 'whats', 'whys' and 'hows' of transforming your words into a published book? If not – prepare to be enlightened. First up, I'd urge you to dispel any preconceived notions you may have about book publishing, because the journey you're about to embark on will be more challenging, but also more rewarding, than you may have imagined. Yet, as with anything in life, the key criteria for success are passion and determination. But before I start expounding the importance of 'finding your passion', let me take you on a short trip down memory lane.

I've always been a lover of books and fascinated by the stories within their pages. Growing up, I lived with my family in a picturesque Sydney suburb overlooking Middle Harbour. Yet, as kids, my brother and I didn't appreciate the beautiful view. Instead, we just bemoaned the fact that our home had very poor television reception, so we missed out on many of the popular television shows our friends watched. Without access to TV, we were forced to discover other pastimes. While my brother enjoyed learning musical instruments and became a talented musician, I discovered the amazing world of books and stories created by writers ... and that passion has remained with me ever since.

Given my love of books, it's not surprising that my career has always involved dealing with words, language and images.

Initially, I worked in libraries and, for a while, it was everything I'd ever wanted in a job. But over time, I became increasingly restless and longed for a change from the Dewey decimal system, covering and repairing books, and endless reshelving. I was ready to head in a new direction. Following a divorce, my self-esteem hit rock bottom and I was motivated to 'shake things up' in my life. So I decided to focus on my long-held dream of studying graphic design and enrolled in a communication and design degree.

After graduating from university, I worked briefly in a marketing role. But right from the start, I knew it wasn't really my 'happy place'. Next, I decided to study a postgraduate course in editing and publishing. It was at this point that a lightbulb went off in my head and everything fell into place; I'd finally discovered what I wanted to be when I grew up! In 2012 I started my own editing and publication design business, Epiphany Editing & Publishing. Then in 2014, I launched my specialist business for indie authors, Brisbane Self Publishing Service … and, as they say, 'the rest is history'.

Fast forward to 2020, when the world was thrown into a state of turmoil and confusion due to the coronavirus pandemic. Everyone was struggling to make sense of the 'new normal'. With more free time on their hands, many people decided to dust off the manuscripts that had been languishing on their computers and work towards getting them published. From my own perspective, I committed to making the most of this period of enforced isolation during lockdown by getting underway with writing this book to document my expertise and knowledge of self-publishing.

I hope you'll find the information I share about how to prepare your book manuscript for publication useful, and I wish you every success on your writing and publishing journey.

Kirsty Ogden, October 2022

Introduction

During the past 30 years, advances in technology have led to massive changes within the publishing industry. Book publishing is currently undergoing a seismic shift, with the rising popularity of self-publishing breaking down the barriers to entry that have always been imposed on emerging writers by traditional publishing houses. In the past, large publishing companies, with their inherent judgement of worthiness and literary merit, were the gatekeepers; a publisher's 'seal of approval' was the only way in for an aspiring author.

But now a grassroots cottage industry is emerging within the publishing world. In their book, *APE – Author, Publisher, Entrepreneur: How to Publish a Book*, Guy Kawasaki and Shawn Welch refer to this new style of book publishing as 'artisanal publishing', whereby writers can control their craft from start to finish. That is, they can exercise control over their book's content, cover, interior design, sales and marketing in much the same way an artisanal bakery or cheesemaker oversees every aspect of their business. This means that authors are now able to bypass large traditional publishers to get their message or story out into the world.

These days, when readers contemplate purchasing a book, they're often unaware who the publisher is. Nevertheless, buyers are just as discerning as they've ever been, and they expect any book they buy to be of high quality. Furthermore, although self-publishing is now a feasible option (particularly for first-time authors), without the legitimacy offered by a traditional publishing company, many writers question the validity of their work and wonder if anyone would be willing to read their story.

While these concerns are legitimate, I can say with absolute certainty that regardless of who you are, what you do or where you come from, you have a story within you that others can benefit from. And if you collaborate with the right people, your story can become a published book. It doesn't matter whether it's based on your personal experiences, or you have a knack for creating tales that transport people to other realms, or you are exceptionally skilled at what you do and want to share your knowledge with the world. In all these scenarios, your written words should be available for other people to enjoy or learn from.

Regardless of the theme or subject area of your book, there are people who will happily pay to read what you have to say. But telling your story in written format is just one phase of that journey. You still need to get your writing published so it can reach a wider audience, and then you'll have to work hard to help them discover your book. Many authors aspire to having a traditional publishing company 'pick up' their book and take on the lion's share of any marketing and distribution activities. But realistically, if you want your story to be out in the world, it's likely you will have to assume responsibility for promoting it yourself, even if your book has been traditionally published.

Now, all this can be very scary if you've never previously published and promoted a book. From developing an initial concept through to writing the draft manuscript, editing the written content, creating the internal page layout and cover design, deciding on the publication formats and then marketing

Introduction

your book, there are so many things you need to consider in order to succeed.

Publishing a book can appear to be simple enough at the outset. However, when you consider such details as book trim size and formats, the administrative aspects (including ISBNs and legal deposit requirements), publishing legalities (including copyright infringement and defamation issues), and the range of distribution options available to authors, achieving your dream of publishing your manuscript can seem overwhelming. When I initially set out to publish this book, my goal wasn't to provide a bullet-point checklist. Instead, I wanted to create a useful guide that would help you understand the self-publishing processes from the first draft of your manuscript through to the stage where your book is ready for readers to enjoy.

Since launching Brisbane Self Publishing Service in 2014, I've spent numerous hours working with many indie authors, helping them to achieve their dream of publishing their book. So I'm aware of the many advantages that self-publishing can offer if you have the right tools and resources at your disposal. Over time, I have developed a proprietary framework (which I've called the Let's Get Published Framework and have registered as an official trademark) to help combat 'overwhelm' and to make all the publishing steps more user-friendly, particularly for first-time authors. My Let's Get Published Framework® encompasses five key book publication stages (i.e. structural editing and/or copyediting, internal page formatting/typesetting, book administration, cover design and proofreading) and offers a useful roadmap for authors to successfully chart their self-publishing journey. I have also created a free email course designed to give aspiring authors a brief insight into the steps involved in publishing their book.

At the outset, I want to emphasise that the self-publishing process can be a minefield and comes with its own set of challenges. But with the right tools, a little motivation, a lot of vision and a team of helpful professionals in your corner, you can scale that mountain and proudly 'raise your book publication flag' for the world to admire. A published book provides an enduring legacy – not just for you and your family but for future generations as well.

So, whether you intend to write and publish just one book or many, this self-publishing resource offers a play-by-play action plan on how to do this while enjoying yourself along the way.

PART ONE

So You Want To Be An Author?

ONE

Before putting words on the page

If you've ever been a fan of reality TV shows like *The X Factor*, you would be aware that while some people are supremely talented and have the ability to deliver a highly professional performance, others make you question the logic behind their decision to get up on stage. And often this isn't because they have no talent; it's the performance itself that feels rushed, unrehearsed and completely out of sync. The difference between an extraordinary performance and a cringeworthy one can come down to preparation.

In the same way, you don't have to be a professional writer in order to get started on the journey to self-publish your book (although, of course, that can be very helpful!). More than anything, you need to ensure that you've prepared yourself mentally for the task ahead. Writing a book doesn't just start when you begin to put words on the page.

This is particularly true if you're keen for your book to be successful in terms of reaching a readership base, creating an income or establishing you as a writer of note within the literary community. If all of these objectives (and more) are on your radar, there are certain things you're going to need to put in place before you even make a start on writing your manuscript. And I'm not talking about developing your story's characters, creating a book outline or deciding on the content you want to include in your book. All of these steps will come further down the track.

At the outset, what is important is laying the proper foundations that will influence your creative processes. This, in turn, will help you develop a better understanding of where to direct your energy and resources in order to achieve your long-term goals.

And speaking of goals, it is crucial for you to be able to clearly define your vision for your book. In the next section, we will explore the concept of setting goals as a writer, because this is critical to the entire publishing process. You want your published book to be like those talent acts that get the judges up on their feet and the crowd cheering the performers on. And that doesn't just happen by accident. There's a lot of preparation that goes on behind the scenes in the months leading up to any professional-quality stage performance.

Thankfully, unlike talent show contestants, you do not need to devote a huge amount of time and energy to mastering a strenuous routine that will only reap rewards for you in the short term. But before you heave a big sigh of relief, you should be aware that, in many ways, the preparation process for writing a book can be just as arduous. However, by following the steps that I'll discuss in this chapter, you can avoid the pitfalls encountered by many writers, so you'll have a better chance of succeeding.

What is your motivation for publishing a book?

Success means different things to different people. As a writer, success might involve becoming a bestselling author, achieving

Chapter 1 – Before putting words on the page

national or international recognition among your peers or, simply, recording your life experiences for your family, friends or local community. Regardless of your definition of success, it is important for you to clearly articulate it to yourself. In other words, before you even start the writing process, you need to be very aware of what outcome you're hoping to achieve. For example:

- What do you envisage for your book's aesthetics?
- How do you want people to feel after reading your book?
- Where would you like your message or story to be shared?

These questions are not intended to create a state of existentialism within you. Think of this process as being like a compass you'd use to help you reach your destination. If you were the captain of a ship and you just set sail without any preconceived idea of the direction you wanted to go, you'd soon find you were wasting valuable resources and eventually you'd become adrift at sea. Your internal compass helps you focus your efforts in order to successfully navigate your path to your final destination. This same principle applies to your publication goals.

Another important benefit of goal-setting is that it helps you avoid distractions that will inevitably occur on your self-publishing journey. Over the years, I have discovered that there are a lot of distractions masked as opportunities (such as quick-fix writing coaching courses) in the world of self-publishing. These gimmicks supposedly offer you solutions to your problems and even a shortcut to achieving your dreams. Yet, in reality, all they do is either slow down your progress or take you completely away from your path. Without a proper game plan, you are more likely to fall for these cheap tricks and, hence, waste valuable time and resources. With this in mind, how do you set goals as a writer so they align with your dream of becoming a published author?

You may already be familiar with the term 'SMART criteria', which involves setting goals and objectives that are specific, measurable, achievable, realistic and time-related. This framework can be a helpful tool for you to establish structure around your writing process. (If you're interested in learning more about the SMART concept, I suggest you check out the Wikipedia description[1].)

I also suggest you jot down your writing and publishing goals and display them in a convenient location (such as taped to your bathroom mirror) where you'll be constantly reminded of what you are working towards. Another important habit that can help you with goal-setting is to break down your big goals into smaller actionable steps that you can execute every day. By taking these small steps, you will steadily progress towards your desired destination. For example, if your goal is to write a book manuscript of 35,000 words within a six-month timeframe, break down the project into achievable daily writing tasks.

When you are clear on what your objectives are, you can then explore the 'hows' of writing your book. In subsequent chapters, we will discuss the practical aspects of achieving your self-publishing goals. This is important in ensuring you are in a good position to determine what approach will work best for you. Even if you decide to hire publishing professionals to oversee your self-publishing project, you still need to be aware of all the available options and how best to collaborate with your 'support team'. This will also make it much easier for you to align your goals with your ultimate vision for your book.

---

1. https://en.wikipedia.org/wiki/SMART_criteria

Identifying the 'why' of your book

Most people who are ambitious and driven to succeed have a clear understanding of why they do what they do. Their 'why' provides the necessary fuel that energises them to pursue their dreams. At the outset, it's important to ask yourself why you want to write a book – or, more specifically, why publishing a book is so important to you. When you are able to answer these questions clearly and with conviction, there should be very little that will stand in your way of achieving your goal.

There are many reasons why people decide to write a book manuscript, and we'll explore a few of them in this chapter. While you read through this section, I suggest that you take some time to clarify your own motivations. They might be based on a desire to connect with others – maybe you have strong views and a conviction about the story you want to share, so you're keen for people to hear your perspective. Whatever your reason, it is important to ensure that it's tangible enough to sustain you when you hit inevitable roadblocks during the writing process.

A lot of writers become motivated to self-publish their manuscripts because they haven't been able to secure book contracts from a traditional publishing company. Many successful authors have had their manuscript rejected numerous times before they were finally able to find a publisher willing to take on their book. However, you may not have sufficient time or patience to endure multiple rejections, so instead, you've resolved to take matters into your own hands and commit to the self-publishing route.

> If you are looking to boost your professional career or establish yourself as an authority in your industry, self-publishing a book can be a great option for you. This path offers a forum for you to share your skills and knowledge with the world, as well as providing answers to some of the problems your clients or other readers might be struggling with. Moreover, you probably already have an audience of potential readers within reach, who will also be happy to spread the word about your book.

One of the most powerful 'whys' that motivates people to self-publish a book is the desire to leave behind a lasting legacy for their family or future generations. A published book can be a good way to share a key event in your life, or even your complete life journey, with others. In previous times, knowledge of our identity and culture were passed on from one generation to another through stories and songs. These days, advances in the printing industry (including the advent of high-quality digital printing) mean that you now have an opportunity to share your personal story in a unique way. Self-publishing a book is an excellent way of sharing your life experiences with friends and family (and possibly even strangers) in your own words.

Understanding the 'why' behind your desire to publish a book can help you develop a clear framework for the writing process. This, in turn, will mean that you will be able to follow through with your milestones for your book publishing project. So, I strongly suggest that you set aside some time early on to figure out your motivations so that you will achieve your publication goals.

Will people be interested in what you have to say?

This is a very tricky question to answer. It's the same as venturing into a new environment for the first time and wondering if people are going to like you. The question here is not really about making your book the best in the world (although, of course, that would be a very desirable goal!) but, rather, about determining its marketability. While many writers want to focus solely on the creative aspect of their craft, if you decide to self-publish a book, you'll also need to consider its sales potential. Consequently, the question, 'Will people be interested in what I have to say?' can serve as a reality check, resulting in an answer that will either support your decision to move forward with your manuscript or prompt you to consider an entirely new angle.

To a large extent, the way in which you answer this question will also determine how you approach the task of writing your manuscript. For example, you may have a topic in mind that you think is a fantastic idea for a book; however, there may be some people who consider the topic to be offensive. If you decide to move forward, any controversy could mean that your book might ultimately end up having limited market appeal. If you want to become a successful author, writing and publishing a book that doesn't resonate with a large section of the market will restrict your sales prospects. So, you need to have a balanced perspective when making decisions about the theme or subject area of your book and its potential impact on readers.

Book marketers and distributors have definite opinions on what type of book genres will be successful in the marketplace. But what they fail to mention is that if you decide to pursue your writing dreams based on a particular genre, your identity as an author is likely to then be defined by that genre. While this may seem to be inconsequential, if you decide you want to head in another direction later on in your writing career, you may struggle to break out of a pigeonhole. For instance, famous author JK Rowling has written several crime/thriller books for adults under the pseudonym Robert Galbraith specifically to avoid pigeonholing and the comparison to her highly acclaimed children's fantasy book series.

Having said that, while I strongly advocate making sure your book will have wide appeal, you shouldn't allow yourself to become overly concerned with what other people think (with the exception of publishing professionals such as editors or literary agents). Some hugely successful books that were published during the writer's lifetime didn't achieve critical acclaim until much later. George Orwell is an example; during his life, his books received much criticism, and it was only later on that people came to appreciate his writing.

What's in a name? Pros and cons of using a pseudonym

As a fledgling writer, you may have contemplated using a pseudonym (or 'pen-name') to self-publish your book. In the past, many well-known authors wrote their manuscripts under pseudonyms in order to conceal their real identities – for example, some women writers adopted male pen-names in the hope of achieving success in what was a very male-dominated field at the time.

If you're considering using a pseudonym for your manuscript, be sure to weigh up all the pros and cons first. This choice will have a significant impact on your journey as an author, so it's a good idea to be well informed before making your final decision.

What are some of the benefits of using a pseudonym, and conversely, what problems could arise from doing so?

Key advantages of using a pseudonym include:
- You can remain anonymous and maintain your privacy (although this is increasingly challenging to do as internet search algorithms become progressively more sophisticated).
- You have the freedom to write about sensitive or controversial topics you may not feel comfortable publishing under your real name.
- You can select a more appealing alternative if your real name is hard to spell/remember/pronounce.
- You create an opportunity to write from a completely different perspective or in a different genre from books you have already published.
- You can reinvent or 'make over' your career as an author if your previous book(s) didn't sell well or were criticised by readers.

While there are benefits associated with using a pen-name, there are also definite disadvantages – in particular, the extra layer of complexity involved in marketing your book. These days, an author needs to promote their book extensively so that potential readers will become aware of it. In this way, your author name – and the face behind it – becomes a form of branding that you need to build on over time.

This means that if you write under a pseudonym, you will have to create a separate, public author identity with separate social media accounts, email address and so on, which involves more work on your part. Moreover, if you want to use multiple pseudonyms for different books or genres, each one will operate like a separate author business, especially if each name represents a vastly different genre or has a distinctive target audience. As a result, your marketing efforts and expenses will exponentially increase. The greater the number of author identities, the greater the cost (both in time and money), which can be overwhelming for one person to manage.

A final point to be aware of if you do decide to publish your book under a pseudonym is that you can't create a false 'persona' around that name. For instance, it is fraudulent to claim you have formal qualifications, experience or education that you don't have in real life. Likewise, if you are guilty of defamation, plagiarism, making false claims or other deceitful activities, your pen-name won't provide any legal protection.

TWO

To write or not to write

Having touched on some of the more esoteric, foundational aspects of your self-publishing journey, we can now move forward to the challenging task of writing your manuscript. At this point, I'll assume that you're 100% committed to writing a book. With the soul-searching and goal-setting steps behind you, it's time to implement your ideas.

If you are time poor or have too many commitments to spend numerous hours writing a manuscript, it is possible for you to delegate the writing task to someone else without losing your claim to the title of author. In this chapter, we'll explore several options for writing your book, including drafting your own manuscript and receiving assistance from a writing professional. (If you do opt for assistance with writing your manuscript, you can choose to be actively involved in the entire process or simply maintain a supervisory role. The extent of your involvement in the project depends on your objectives and also your budget.) We'll also investigate various tools and resources that are available to help you to produce a high-quality manuscript. And finally, we'll deal with the pesky problem of writer's block and how you can overcome it.

You're not alone: ghostwriting and writing coaching

There are several methods of writing your book manuscript, the two most common being to write it completely yourself or to have someone else write it but assign credit to you (these people are called 'ghostwriters'). There are numerous benefits to writing your manuscript yourself; however, hiring someone else to write your book also has its advantages. You just need to figure out what your strengths are and what approach works best for you.

For example, if writing is not something you have done before and you are a business owner with many calls on your time, it may be more practical (and ultimately more economical) for you to engage the services of a professional ghostwriter. If you attempted to take on the task of writing your manuscript yourself, you'd possibly waste a lot of time, resources and energy without achieving a good outcome, whereas hiring a ghostwriter would free you up to focus on outlining your ideas for your book. A professional ghostwriter would then be able to follow through on these ideas to create the structural framework and content for your book.

Another factor that can influence the book-writing process is the level of your personal and work commitments. Without any prior experience, it's easy to feel overwhelmed by the scope of the writing project and its associated deadlines. So rather than having to cope with that kind of pressure, it may be easier to commission a professional to help you get your book manuscript written within your desired timeframe.

The next step, then, involves finding a reputable ghostwriter for your book-writing project. Many freelancer websites are available, and some of them (such as Reedsy, Writer Finder and Upwork) offer top-rated ghostwriters and content writers who specialise in different subject areas. So whether you'd simply like to get a professional writer to build on your basic book concept or you want to hire someone with a background in your speciality or subject area, I suggest you spend some time initially researching different options online.

> To help you find the best person for your writing project, ask your colleagues or other authors for word-of-mouth recommendations, or consider collaborating with a self-publishing services company. These businesses usually have an established network of publishing professionals, so they may be able to put you in touch with a ghostwriter who is well suited to your project.

If you are a more experienced writer, or you have more time available, or you have insufficient financial resources to hire a ghostwriter, then writing your manuscript yourself is the best scenario. Nevertheless, you may find this route challenging because your ideas do not flow as freely as you would like them to or you struggle to remain motivated for the duration of the writing process. For these (and many more) reasons, engaging the services of a writing coach can be a helpful approach.

A writing coach is the middle ground between hiring a ghostwriter and writing your manuscript completely by yourself. It's like working with a personal trainer, only in this case the focus is on your writing skills and timelines. Depending on the budget you've set aside for your project, you may decide to hire a writing coach from the start or, alternatively, wait until you hit a point where you feel you need some professional support to overcome a particular roadblock. A writing coach can help you develop a structural framework for your manuscript and motivate you to stick to your book project timelines.

Both of these approaches to writing your book manuscript have their advantages and, of course, disadvantages. Deciding which one suits you will depend on such factors as your budget and overall objectives for your book. However, I should mention here that budget doesn't just mean the financial costs associated with your project; it also means your available time and your mental/emotional resources. So before you commit to either method, determine which one will help you achieve your goal in the most effective way without excessively draining your reserves.

Establishing timelines for your writing project

When it comes to setting timelines for your book-writing project, there are two aspects for you to consider:

- The first timeline relates to the duration of your entire writing project, from the point where you dream up your ideas through to fleshing out your book's framework and then finally producing a completed manuscript.
- The second timeline relates to the sequence in which events occur in your book (this is particularly important if you are writing a fiction or narrative-style non-fiction book).

In this section, we will examine the first type of timeline: how you can set reasonable targets for your book project deliverables. Then, the second type of timeline – reviewing the actual narrative arc of your book's storyline or structure – will be discussed in chapter 3.

Writing a book can take anything from a few weeks to a few years to accomplish. There are no established guidelines to refer to that determine when a manuscript should be completed, as there are many factors to consider. When setting the timeframe for writing your manuscript, such factors as your goal and/or vision for your book, the total word count and your level of preparedness can influence the duration of the project. You also need to understand that the project milestones you set are influenced by the publishing professionals you work with, as well as your tenacity in driving the project forward. Regardless, given how easy it is to become derailed or distracted from writing a book, it is a good idea to establish some firm boundaries for your project deadline.

Setting a final deadline for your self-publishing project involves establishing an immovable end date. This could be the date you want your manuscript to be ready to send to an editor. It should be a non-negotiable date that you've resolved not to postpone or cancel. Consider this deadline carefully, as it needs to be realistic and allow sufficient time for all the steps to be taken between now and then. It could be in five or six months (or more) from where you are right now.

Whatever you decide on, this firm deadline will be your D-day. You can now backtrack from the deadline to where you currently are and plan each of your project milestones accordingly. Give yourself some 'wriggle room' of about a fortnight prior to your D-day to accommodate any last-minute changes. Plan out the entire writing project and set up milestones so you can track your progress and make any adjustments where necessary. Determine how much time you are willing to commit every day to writing your manuscript. When you have completed this brainstorming task, note the milestones on your calendar so you will know how far you need to have progressed every week with your manuscript to reach your goal.

Some tips for navigating common writing pitfalls

There was a time when the stereotypical image of a writer was of an intense-looking person hunched over an old-fashioned typewriter with a mug of coffee beside them. However, while the mug of coffee might still be just as important, these days many great tools and resources are available to make the process of writing a book much easier than tapping away on a clunky typewriter. Tools such as Scrivener, Evernote and Google Docs can make the writing process faster and simpler, as well as more cohesive for collaborative projects. But in this section, our focus won't be on the actual writing tools. Rather, I'll share some writing tips that can help enhance your success as a writer. With experience – as well as input from experts like editors and proofreaders – you will gradually develop a deeper understanding of best practice for writers.

Below are some useful tips to help you navigate potential problems and succeed in your writing practice.

1. Be kind to yourself

Writers are frequently their own harshest critics and, due to a tendency to perfectionism, can often struggle with their work and/or their overall wellbeing. This unfortunate personality trait means they often focus on the negatives rather than the positives.

If you're going to succeed as a writer, it's important for you to be kind to yourself. Ensure you structure your daily and weekly routine so you have plenty of opportunity for relaxation and down time, in addition to factoring in time for your writing work.

2. Read other authors' books

Good writers tend to be prolific readers. The reality is that most writers are shaped by the work of other authors. Of course, this doesn't mean that it's alright to directly copy another writer's words. Instead, open yourself up to the influence of other writers' perspectives by reading widely, and be willing to explore new genres beyond those you usually gravitate towards.

3. Art first, money later

If you are writing a book because you are hoping to become a millionaire, you might want to rethink your plans as this is probably not the best endeavour for you. This doesn't mean that making money from selling your book can't be one of your publication goals nor that it's an impossible goal for you to achieve. It simply means that when you put money first, it can have a negative impact on your creativity due to potential constraints on your freedom of expression.

4. Have a professional editor on speed dial

Often, the difference between a good writer and a great writer is their editor. An editor is a skilful professional who can help you improve the technical aspects of your writing and, at the same time, support your creative vision. Editing is an essential ingredient in your recipe for creating a high-quality book. If you have decided to self-publish your manuscript and are keen to undertake all the stages yourself, this is an important step that you shouldn't skimp on.

5. Master the art of juggling

For many people, writing is something they do on the side or in their spare time on top of juggling a full-time job or home or caring responsibilities. But writing can be very demanding and requires both endurance and commitment. So, to ensure one aspect of your life doesn't suffer at the expense of another, you'll need to learn to juggle successfully. Set aside time in your weekly schedule for writing and ensure you prioritise these times so you stay on task with your book project.

How to overcome writer's block

Unfortunately, writer's block is a common challenge for many authors. At some point on your writing journey, your words may stop flowing. Instead, you may spend hours staring at a blank screen without any idea of how to move forward with your manuscript.

Writer's block can strike for many reasons. For instance:

- You might be under pressure in your personal or work life, and the timing for writing your book isn't right for you at the moment.
- You might be a perfectionist and be imposing unrealistically high expectations on yourself. In other words, you have an idea of what you want your writing to sound like, but you're not able to adequately translate your thoughts onto the page in a cohesive and engaging manner.
- You might be suffering from self-doubt and feel like you are an impostor.

If things aren't currently in balance in your life, you may be well advised to set aside your writing task for a while and pick up where you've left off a little further down the track. But don't allow this to become an excuse for completely derailing your project. Entertaining these thoughts will not only have a negative impact on your timelines but also make it difficult for you to continue with your writing project when the time is right.

Many writers undervalue their creativity and aren't aware of their unique skills and talent. For them, writing is nothing special – it's just what they do. Viewing their writing with a perfectionist's eye, they see all kinds of flaws that are invisible to others. While it is important to strive to produce high-quality work, perfectionism can become a stumbling block that stops you having sufficient belief in yourself to complete your writing project.

If self-doubt and impostor syndrome are stopping your writing from progressing, you may need to spend some time focusing on developing skills that boost your confidence. In her book, *The Successful Author Mindset: A Handbook for Surviving the Writer's Journey*, Joanna Penn shares that, like many other high-profile and prolific authors, she regularly struggles with feeling like an impostor. She also advises new writers to embrace self-doubt as part of the creative process.

Unfortunately, there is no magic wand that will quickly dispel writer's block. Most likely, you'll have to find out what works for you through trial and error. But regardless of the cause, you shouldn't just try to plough through if you are experiencing writer's block. Instead, you can try several methods to get your creative juices flowing again. These include:

- Reciting self-motivating affirmations every day to help you stay on track.
- Setting aside your manuscript for a while and distracting yourself with something else. If you enjoy being outdoors, for instance, then getting out into nature and going for a long walk might reinspire you to write.
- Focusing on hobbies such as painting, cooking, sewing, knitting or other creative activities to free up your imagination.
- Working on yourself (possibly with professional assistance from a therapist or life coach) to resolve any emotional roadblocks that impede you from making progress with your manuscript. (This process can help you uncover gems of inspiration which, in turn, can improve your writing skills in the longer term.)

- Engaging the services of a writing coach to show you how to unlock the source of your current barrier, as well as supporting you to develop creative solutions to combat the problem.

Sharing is caring: writers' groups, retreats and workshops

One big downside of writing is that it can be a very lonely experience. While solitude is essential in order for you to get the task done, it's important to find opportunities to connect with other writers who share the same aspirations and dreams as you do. Collaborating with publishing professionals who work closely with you on your book project will also keep you motivated to reach the finish line. These interactions will stimulate your creativity, as well as provide practical tips and resources to help you deal with any challenges on your writing and publishing journey.

These days, the internet has become our main source of information when conducting research for a book or other work and/or personal reasons. However, exchanging information with real people on a one-on-one basis can be equally (if not more) effective. In addition to finding out specific answers to your writing questions, you can benefit from their practical know-how. Interacting with real people can also stop you from feeling isolated and presuming that any writing challenges you're facing are unique to you. Discovering that other people also struggle with the same issues makes it much easier to cope with any setbacks you're currently experiencing.

Connecting with other writers via writers' groups, retreats and/or workshops can boost your confidence and help you to forge new bonds that will support you throughout your writing practice. Let's face it: only other writers who share similar

Chapter 2 – To write or not to write

experiences can fully relate to and empathise with your journey. But I think one of the most profound benefits of this form of collaboration is that it can reignite your passion for writing.

So instead of viewing the writing task as a chore that needs to be checked off your to-do list, discover new ways to enjoy the process. This, in turn, will invigorate your creative spark and reconnect you to the 'why' that underpins your desire to publish your book.

THREE

How to write it right

Many writers (particularly first-time writers) have a tendency to perfectionism. From the very first word through to the final punctuation mark, they want their draft manuscript to look and sound a specific way, and they'll spend a huge amount of time trying to achieve it. If you find yourself obsessing over the typefaces, language or tone of your book, then welcome to the perfectionists' club! Given that you are staking your future as a writer on your book manuscript, your concerns that it should be as perfect as possible are valid and completely understandable. But rather than biting your nails and pulling out your hair obsessing over minor details, let's consider some practical and actionable steps that will help allay your fears.

Writing a high-quality book goes beyond having a perfect draft manuscript that is free from any grammatical errors or typos. Remember, working with a professional editor during the editing phase of your book publishing project will help you to polish your writing so it sparkles! Instead, *your* task is to focus on creating the content so that your published book will engage your ideal readers and potentially educate, persuade and/or entertain them. In this chapter, I'll outline how you can harness various writing techniques to help get your ideas out of your head and onto the page while also keeping your final publishing goals firmly in mind.

Pinpointing your book's core theme or message

Having already defined your writing vision and goals, you are probably well aware of whether you will publish a fiction or non-fiction manuscript. So the next step is to focus on the subject area or theme of your book.

> **Pinpointing the core theme or message of your book will help you to determine the key information you need to include in your manuscript. This tactic applies to all types of genres and topics.**

Possibly you've decided you want to write a fiction manuscript. If that's the case, what's its genre? Will it be a romance, horror, crime/mystery, fantasy or science fiction book? Next, you will need to refine this even further to clarify your book's sub-genre. For example, if you are going to write a romance book, will it be a historical period romance that takes your readers back to a previous era? Or would you prefer to write a contemporary romantic comedy or 'chick-lit' manuscript where readers can imagine themselves being active participants in the storyline?

The theme of a novel usually relates to the 'life lesson' the hero or main character must learn or discover before the end of the book. In this way, as well as the 'external' story or main plot of the novel, there should also be an 'internal' story – a personal journey of transformation for the protagonist. Consider basing your theme around your protagonist's central flaw and how they are transformed by the events in the story. What do they really need in order to learn their lesson, and how does the story get them there? Readers need to witness the central character undergoing personal growth or transformation.

While the purpose of non-fiction writing is to provide an accurate and truthful depiction of ideas, facts and events, this writing style can also have a powerful emotional impact on readers, as well as teaching them something new. For instance, the universal themes of love and friendship, family, courage and personal growth are common aspects of narrative non-fiction books such as memoirs and biographies.

As well as identifying the core theme of your book, it's important to consider the best approach to highlighting this concept via the narrative framework of your manuscript. If you are writing a fiction manuscript, you will need to create a book timeline, as we've already considered in chapter 2. The sequences in which each character appears and their relationship to each other is integral to the entire concept of your book's story or narrative. For example, you need to keep in mind the age a character was when a certain event occurred and the timeframe that has elapsed since they moved on to the next phase in the storyline ... and so on. Ensuring that you have your time sequences correct is vital because it helps you focus only on those events that are relevant to your story.

If you are writing a non-fiction book, deciding on an initial framework (possibly in the form of a table of contents) will help you to determine what to include in your book. People read non-fiction books with a specific purpose in mind. They are seeking information they can use, understand and relate to, so you should make it your mission to express your ideas clearly and write with authority. As the author of a non-fiction book, you want your readers to be willing to stick around long enough to engage with your ideas. For that to happen, you'll need to pique their interest from the first page and keep the momentum going until the last page. Your book should fulfil your promise to your reader to either entertain them or educate them ... or both.

Once you've decided on the theme of your book, the next step is ensuring your text is accurate and authentic. Research extensively to educate yourself and learn as much as possible about the genre or subject area in which you write so your book won't contain any embarrassing errors that will reduce your credibility in the eyes of readers. For instance, if you're going to write a historical Scottish Highlands romance, it is important for you to delve into that particular country and era to understand the cultural norms of the time period. This will help you to determine how your characters would have spoken and interacted with each other, as well as their style of dress, the type of food they ate and any other distinctive customs of that location and era. Even if you are writing a memoir, you still need to undertake some background research into aspects of your own life to be able to recall, verify and describe significant details of people, places and events from your past.

The more research you undertake during the initial writing stages, the more adept you will be at painting a vivid picture in readers' minds. If you are a fiction author, you may be keen to use your imagination to create an entire fictional universe. In this case, your descriptions of this fantasy world need to be plausible in order for your scenes to seem convincing to readers. A renowned example of a detailed fictional universe is Arda (more popularly known as Middle-earth), which JRR Tolkien created for his books *The Lord of the Rings*, *The Hobbit* and *The Silmarillion*. Narnia is another well-known mythical world, created by CS Lewis and presented in his seven-part children's fantasy series, *The Chronicles of Narnia*. While you may not be able to achieve the same level of imaginative clarity in your own descriptions as these famous authors, there are certain things you can do to improve the quality of your writing.

Characteristics of a successful fiction book

An important 'home truth' about being an author is that it's unlikely your book will appeal to everyone. No matter how talented or creative you may be as a writer, there will always be those people who read your work and shrug their shoulders indifferently. But take heart and don't abandon your publishing dreams just yet as there are many things you can do that will have a positive impact on your book's reception with readers. For non-fiction authors, the writing process associated with producing a successful book has some minor differences compared to the process for fiction authors. However, the core elements involved in creating an effective narrative are still basically the same for both categories. You just need to find an angle that will suit your book.

The opening

Every book should have an opening scene that immediately grabs the reader's attention. The first page or so of your book will determine how the rest of the story will play out and whether or not people are willing to commit to reading it. Think of a movie you've seen that you really enjoyed. Maybe within the first few minutes, there was a dramatic or intriguing scene that thrilled you and, at the same time, made you curious about how the storyline would continue. This strategy ties in with a common technique that writers use: a flashback or flash forward. They will skip forward to a drama-filled scene that may appear to be completely unrelated to the first few chapters of the narrative and use this as the opening of their book. This type of dramatic tension helps engage an audience's emotions, reeling them in so they feel motivated to continue watching the movie or reading the book.

The characters

Your story is only as good as the characters that inhabit it. This is because your readers will experience the story you have written through the eyes of your characters. Therefore, it is important for you to create believable characters who have multiple facets to their personalities. For example, the villain in your story shouldn't simply be the 'bad guy'. Strive to create an emotional connection between your reader and this villain. Readers should be able to understand where the villain is coming from ... though this shouldn't stop readers from hating them (or even secretly loving them). In the same vein, your hero should be more than just the morally upright 'good guy'. You also need to highlight their character flaws and make them seem as human as possible. The amount of attention you give to developing your characters will play out in your narrative arc and help to ensure your readers remain invested in your storyline.

The storyline

Compelling characters require a compelling storyline. You need to create a plot that reels your readers in, moving them through the story to reach a crescendo of dramatic tension between the characters and/or their situation, hitting the climax and then bringing them back 'down to earth' with the drama being resolved. Generally speaking, creating a convincing storyline doesn't happen by simply 'winging it'. You need to be strategic during the writing process so you're aware of the number of events that need to take place within the plotline even before you commit this information to the page. Creating a timeline that drives the events of your narrative will ensure your readers remain engaged from the first page to the last page of your book.

The dialogue

Regardless of how much you focus on describing your characters' unique attributes, nothing showcases their personalities as much as their speech. Your ability to reveal the experiences of your characters through their dialogue is crucial to bringing those characters to life. Pay close attention to the language each of your characters uses to ensure that no two sound exactly alike. This will add texture and an extra layer of authenticity to the story you are creating for your readers. However, a narrative that consists entirely of dialogue can become monotonous and boring. You should aim for a balance of dialogue, description and exposition to carry your reader effortlessly along with your book's storyline.

Crafting the perfect non-fiction book title and subtitle

For non-fiction writers, it's important to give careful consideration to the title and subtitle for your book, because these elements are key for marketing it. In other words, you shouldn't just opt for a creative or clever option; you want the title to be memorable so readers will notice your published book among all the others, but you also want it to be informative so they can immediately tell if your book is relevant to their needs.

Many people search for non-fiction books with a specific theme or subject area in mind or to find answers to a specific problem. For example, self-help books (such as diet or health books) usually contain research data, motivational techniques and practical strategies for readers to follow in order to improve certain aspects of their lives. Consequently, if you focus solely on crafting a book title that appeals to your artistic sensibilities rather than one that reflects your book's content, you will probably end up losing potential readers. This is because when readers are searching online or in a 'bricks and mortar' bookshop, they're quite likely to bypass your book without realising it's actually what they're looking for. So make sure you take a strategic approach to crafting the title for your book.

An effective book title has three core attributes:

- First, the title needs to grab readers' attention when they are browsing online or in a bookshop so they stop in their tracks, investigate further and hopefully decide to buy the book. When I talk about grabbing readers' attention, I'm not just referring to the visual aspect of your book's cover; we will explore the design stage later on. What I'm actually referring to here is the words you use. Try to come up with a combination of words that will 'speak to' the needs of the reader and encourage them to consider your book as a possible solution to their problem or pain point.

- Second, the title and subtitle need to convey what the book is about. The KISS (keep it simple, stupid) approach is useful for deciding on an effective title and subtitle for your book. In this way, rather than trying to think of clever or slick wording to describe a how-to book, you simply use a straightforward no-frills title. For example, if you have written a manuscript to educate people about how to write an effective business proposal, you could simply call your book, *How to Draft Business Proposals*.

- Third, the title should be easy to say without causing any embarrassment or awkwardness. If a book's title is hard to pronounce or, more importantly, includes words that sound ridiculous when said aloud, people are less likely to buy it and also less inclined to spread the word about it.

For most non-fiction authors, a good technique for selecting an effective title is to use a short title (usually fewer than five or six words) and a longer descriptive subtitle. A well-known example of a catchy non-fiction book title with a descriptive subtitle is Robert T Kiyosaki's book, *Rich Dad Poor Dad: What the Rich Teach Their Kids About Money That the Poor and Middle Class Do Not!* Another good example is Brian Tracy's book *Eat That Frog! 21 Great Ways to Stop Procrastinating and Get More Done in Less Time*.

To figure out a good option for your book's title and subtitle, focus on the key problem you are trying to solve for readers and the unique solution you are offering them. Spending some time brainstorming the title and subtitle for your book will help to ensure it gains traction in the marketplace. Try to come up with multiple titles and subtitles and then choose the version you think best represents your writing style and the content of your book.

General writing rules (and whether it's okay to break them)

In my experience, writers tend to be strong-minded individuals who like to 'row their own boat' and follow their creative impulses. When it comes to the rules of writing, my approach is to simply suggest them as helpful guidelines rather than rigid dictates. Over the years, I have witnessed many writers (particularly fiction authors) defy these rules and publish books that are well received by readers. This is not to say you should set out to flout every grammar rule or language convention when writing your manuscript, but you also don't need to rigidly adhere to them. Discover your own rhythm and then stick with what works best for you. But at the outset it is important for you to be aware of English language conventions. So on the following two pages, I've outlined a few basic rules that can act as guidelines for your writing journey.

1. Use active voice rather than passive voice

'Voice' is a grammatical term that refers to whether the subject of the sentence is acting or receiving the action of the verb. Using active voice can considerably improve your writing style. Active voice makes your writing more interesting and livelier, so it has greater impact on readers. In contrast, passive voice can make your writing seem stilted and overly formal. It also creates a feeling of distance between the writer and the reader. Check out the following example.

- *Active voice:* Ian kicked the football.
  (In this sentence, the subject is Ian. You can picture Ian kicking the ball while being totally absorbed in this activity. The sentence is alive and interesting.)

- *Passive voice:* The football was kicked by Ian.
  (When the sentence is constructed in this way, the subject is the football. The sense of action is gone, and the emphasis has shifted from the subject *performing* the action to the subject *receiving* the action. It is not so easy to visualise what is happening, and so the sentence seems dull and boring.)

2. Avoid clichés

Clichés are phrases or opinions that are overused, and they demonstrate a lack of original thought in writing. While they can sometimes be useful to convey a simple message, they're usually just tired and worn-out expressions. When we read clichés, our eyes often skip over them, because they are too familiar and so they have very little impact. We also tend to make a mental note that the author has not been creative or used their own style of writing, so they probably can't be taken seriously. Your writing should be clear, original and free from clichés to ensure that your narrative is engaging for readers.

3. Construct your sentences using strong verbs

Verbs help to bring your writing to life. When you use verbs effectively, you galvanise the dynamism in your narrative and engage people's imagination. As a result, your reader can 'peer behind the curtain' and become immersed in the story you are telling. If you can master this technique, your writing will be lively and more fluid, which, in turn, makes it more rewarding for readers.

When constructing your sentences, try to find strong verbs to use instead of weak verbs plus adverbs. Let's consider an example of this.

- *The giant **walked slowly** across the road.*
  (In this sentence, the adverb 'slowly' describes how the giant walked, but it doesn't convey a strong sense of what the giant looked like while crossing the road.)
- *The giant **lumbered** across the road.*
  (In this version, 'lumbered' conjures a much more vivid image of the giant crossing the road clumsily or heavily because of their bulk.)

Also, look out for overuse of 'nominalisation' in your writing (especially if you're writing non-fiction). This refers to the practice of making nouns out of verbs and is done by adding endings such as *-ation*, *-ility*, *-ance* and *-ment* to verbs. Here are a few examples and how to change them back into verbs:

- take into consideration → consider
- is in alignment with → aligns with
- to be ignorant of → to ignore

Also called 'verbal nouns', these words tend to drain the life out of a sentence and reduce reader engagement.

4. Pay attention to tense and point of view (POV)

At the outset, you need to decide whether you will write your manuscript using past or present tense, and also determine which point of view (POV) to use. POV refers to which person or character is telling or narrating a story or other piece of writing – that is, from whose perspective the reader discovers what is going on. POV can be first person (*I* and *we* pronouns), second person (*you* pronouns) or third person (*he*, *she*, *it* and *they* pronouns). Third person POV can be either omniscient, where the narrator knows what all the characters are doing in the story, or limited to only a specific character's experience.

Unless you want to incorporate a change in time period or context within your manuscript, you should keep tenses and perspectives consistent. If you inadvertently switch between tenses and viewpoints, you'll confuse many of your readers. Of course, some books are purposefully written across multiple timelines or from multiple perspectives. So if this is the case with yours, make sure you use the right tense or POV at the right time.

Author's voice, style and tone: what are they, and how do you identify yours?

An author's 'voice' is the manner in which they tell a story. In the same way that a piece of music sounds quite different played on a violin compared to a flute (or a song is sung by a choir or a rapper), a story with the exact same plot, characters or setting can seem very different depending on the author's voice. Developing your author's voice helps to establish a writing mode that is uniquely your own. For many authors, their 'voice' is exactly the same way that they talk. Over time, the tone, style and structure of an author's writing may evolve into something that is a completely unique expression of their personality on the page.

'Style' is defined as the specific way in which we create, perform or do something. For an author, style is the way in which they use words to tell a story. Your writing style will be personal to you and simply indicates to the reader that this written content is *your* handiwork. It's not something you are taught in school; in fact, you may not even realise that you have a distinctive writing style. In the same way that someone puts together items of clothing and jewellery or applies make-up to create a personal style, the way in which a person assembles words and sentences forms their writing style.

Whenever you vividly describe a situation, you will tend to use certain words and sentence structures consistently for that description; that's your style. It might be described as articulate, conversational, formal, businesslike, flowery, literary, rambling or poetic. Your writing style may also showcase a specific genre or subject area where you naturally shine. On the flip side, your writing style may become a crutch you rely on too heavily. You may find yourself repeating the same phrases over and over and not be aware of this writing 'tic'. This is another reason you should always work with a professional editor – they will review your written work and point out any blind-spots you may have.

'Tone' refers to an author's use of words and writing style to convey their attitude towards a subject. What the *author* feels about a particular topic is often defined as the tone, whereas what the *reader* feels is known as the 'mood'. Essentially, your tone is how you convey your underlying message. It might be humorous, sarcastic, unhappy, nostalgic … the list is endless. This is an important concept to grasp because it plays an essential role in determining the way someone is likely to feel after reading your book

Let's use this book as an example. When I first set out to write my manuscript, my aim was to educate first-time authors by sharing my experience and knowledge of the steps involved in writing and publishing their book. However, I didn't want the book to be overly formal and contain lots of facts and references. My goal is for writers to enjoy reading the content, as well as gleaning valuable book publishing information along the way. So, I have tried to ensure my written words sound like we are having a conversation. My intention is for you to feel as though I am speaking to you directly and guiding you on your self-publishing journey.

* * *

Having explored the ins and outs of writing your manuscript, let's now move forward to consider the first key step in publishing a high-quality book: the editing stage.

PART TWO

Editing Basics For Flawless Content

FOUR

Your foundational editing checklist

As an author, you've spent a lot of time working on your draft manuscript and know your written content inside out. But will your readers understand what you mean, or will they be confused by your words? At this point, it's time to consider the next step in your publishing journey: the editing process.

Editing your manuscript should not be an optional extra in your book project game plan. Research has shown that even trivial mistakes can result in a reader questioning the standard of an author's work. Incorrect spelling, punctuation and grammar may not only cause confusion, but also distract readers from the original message so that they decide to look elsewhere for the information they need.

It can be helpful to think of writing a book as being a similar creative activity to making a movie. In the case of a movie production, there is the scriptwriter (or multiple scriptwriters) who creates the overall storyline and dialogue, the actors who bring the characters to life, and the director who has an overarching concept of the narrative and captures it on screen. As the author of your book, you take on all of these roles. You create the structure of your manuscript, you bring the characters to life with words that describe the scenes and form their dialogue, and you direct the story to share your vision with your reading audience. With a movie, the film editors are responsible for pulling the scenes together so that everything works harmoniously to present the story for viewers' enjoyment. Likewise, a book editor can help an author to polish their manuscript to ensure it becomes the best published book it can possibly be, ready to entice readers.

In the same way that a movie is unlikely to be successful if the editors assemble the filmed scenes together without adding transitions, music, special effects and everything else that captures viewers' attention, the editing stage is not optional if you want your published book to be of high quality. You can undertake a basic self-edit of your draft manuscript if you are willing to invest time into this process, and it will certainly improve the book – but only so far, because you are too close to your own written work and can't be objective. Alternatively, as soon as you've completed the writing process, you can hire a professional editor to polish your draft manuscript. If you have limited funds, I strongly recommend you do both. A professional editor won't have to put as much work into editing your manuscript if you have already spent time fixing any typos, grammatical errors or unnecessarily long-winded descriptions yourself.

There are a range of applications and software programs (such as Grammarly and PerfectIt) that use artificial intelligence (commonly known as 'AI') to review written text. However, none of them are 100% effective, as there are certain things computers are simply not equipped to do. This is because editing is about much more than correcting text; it also involves understanding the creative nuances and subtleties of language. So if you're planning to rely solely on using software applications to review your manuscript, you might want to reconsider this approach in order to get the best possible outcome.

> When you are creating your book project timeline, make sure you set aside time to self-edit your written text. This will give you an opportunity to carefully scan your content for any mistakes you will have missed during the initial writing stage.

But before you launch into self-editing your manuscript, it's important to understand exactly what you need to look out for. In the following sections I'll explain what's involved if you are going to self-edit your book or if you want to hire a professional editor to polish your writing … or if you decide to do both.

Self-editing and working with beta readers

As the name implies, 'self-editing' involves spending time manually reviewing your own writing. In contrast, beta readers are people who will read your manuscript and provide you with some initial feedback. However, beta readers should not be mistaken for professional editors. There is a world of difference between a beta reader and a professional editor, which we will explore later on in this chapter. For now, it's helpful to be aware that both self-editing and using beta readers are excellent options if you have a very limited budget but are still keen to improve your draft manuscript. (At this stage, you may also be interested in reading developmental editor Tiffany Yates Martin's excellent book on this topic, *Intuitive Editing: A Creative and Practical Guide to Revising Your Writing*.)

There are both pros and cons associated with self-editing your book manuscript. One of the obvious pros is that it doesn't cost you any money; however, it will end up costing you time and effort. You should be mindful that when you self-edit your writing, you tend to miss errors and/or key information because you are familiar with the manuscript and what you are trying to say. Readers (particularly if they aren't already conversant with your subject area) may be confused if there is any missing information when they read your book. This is why it is helpful to get feedback from an outside source such as a beta reader.

'Beta reader' is just a fancy term for anyone you know who is willing to read your book and share their (honest!) thoughts with you. Ideally, a beta reader will act as a 'test' reader who comments on your written content and offers their opinion about your book. They may tell you what is missing from your narrative or how they think you could improve your manuscript from an average reader's perspective. This can help you to fix issues that you may not have previously noticed because you are too close to your own work. While a friend, a colleague at work or a member of your family may be happy to read your first-draft manuscript, the reality is that they are likely to be generally positive and less critical about your written work. Alternatively, some enthusiastic readers of a particular genre or subject area may happily review your manuscript, or if you belong to a writing group, several people might work together to appraise what you've written and suggest ways you could improve it. Getting another independent perspective can be very helpful, and many authors use beta readers to help them enhance their writing.

But as I mentioned previously, it's important not to confuse the different roles that beta readers and editors play in the publishing process. Although beta readers can help you to improve

Chapter 4 – Your foundational editing checklist

your manuscript initially, they don't usually have expertise in, and knowledge of, the three stages of editing (i.e. structural editing, copyediting and proofreading) that a professional editor offers. In fact, you may decide to hire an editor to undertake a professional assessment or critique of your manuscript instead of – or as well as – engaging a beta reader.

Now that we have differentiated between self-editing and beta readers, let's explore the process of reviewing your manuscript yourself, including some tips to make this process simpler and more efficient for you. As I mentioned previously, editing doesn't simply involve using the spelling and grammar checking tools that are bundled up with your word processing software. Although these tools can be very useful, they have their limitations.

When you self-edit your writing, you should read through your manuscript carefully and slowly, checking your written text for accuracy, repetition, consistency and flow. Below is more information about each of these four key concepts to consider:

- *Accuracy* – Ensure you are using the correct words and spelling throughout your manuscript. Also, check grammatical aspects of your text, including using full stops and capital letters when a sentence ends and another one starts. Margaret Ramsay's book, *The Complete Guide to English Usage for Australian Students* is a helpful resource if you need to brush up your knowledge of English grammar.
- *Repetition* – Sentences, phrases or words that are repeated can deter people from wanting to continue reading your book. Once something is stated, such as a character's physical description, it does not need to be mentioned again unless used for emphasis or to progress the story in some way. And even then, instead of repeating the same details, it's a good idea to 'mix

things up' by weaving the characters' physical attributes into the narrative in a variety of ways. Also, if you notice the same words or phrases are cropping up in your writing (particularly on the same page or paragraph), make sure you change them. If necessary, use a thesaurus to find synonyms for a particular word.

- *Consistency* – When you pick a style or tense, such as first person and present tense, make sure you stick to it throughout your manuscript. Note down the spelling of character names, places, particular words and relevant terms so that you use the same spelling throughout your book.

- *Flow* – To check your writing flows well, read your manuscript out loud from beginning to end. This will help you identify any sentences or ideas that don't sound quite right or are too wordy, hard to read or jarring. You should be able to read your sentences without any abrupt stops or interruptions, and your text should be smooth and easy to read. You can achieve this by having natural transitions between sentences and ensuring the paragraphs follow a logical order.

Editing and proofreading: how do they differ?

Before I move on to discussing the three stages of editing in detail, it is important to first clear up any misconceptions you may have about the terms 'editing' and 'proofreading'. Most people use these two words interchangeably, but they actually refer to two very different stages of the editing process. Depending on the overall condition of your written manuscript, the editing stage is often the most time-consuming step in the publishing process, whereas proofreading is the final check after your Word manuscript has been typeset and before it is published.

Editing (particularly structural or developmental editing) is a much more complex process than proofreading, and it can take weeks (and sometimes even months) for an editor to complete one project. Structural editing considers the big-picture perspective, focusing on the organisation and presentation of the manuscript rather than grammar, punctuation and spelling. In contrast, during the copyediting phase, an editor will focus on the details of the written text, reviewing it for style, language, clarity, sentence structure, syntax, word choice, consistency and readability. An editor may also include suggestions (in the form of Track Changes and Comments in the Word manuscript) regarding rewriting certain sections, and/or reorganising the sentence or paragraph structure of your draft manuscript.

Proofreading is the final 'quality control' phase of the editing process. It occurs after the structural and/or copyediting phases have been completed (and you have responded to the editor's suggested edits and comments) and the edited manuscript has been typeset. It is the proofreader's job to review the final copy of the typeset manuscript for any minor typos, grammatical issues or formatting mistakes prior to the book being printed. Proofreaders work through a typeset PDF file – word by word and page by page – checking all aspects of the book layout, including spaces between words and lines, indentations, typeface style, page numbers, consistency of headers and footers, image and table captions, and so on. The proofreading stage is not the time for revisiting any major issues with the manuscript or rewriting the text, as that should have already been addressed during the previous editing stages.

Structural editing: the big-picture perspective

Structural editing involves taking a big-picture approach to evaluating both non-fiction and fiction book manuscripts. Sometimes referred to as 'developmental' or 'substantive' editing, this form of editing is the most time-consuming but also the most creative stage of the editing process.

During the structural edit, an editor will consider any organisational and content issues within the manuscript. For organisational issues, they will suggest how you could rework your content so the final book has a more coherent format, progression and flow. Where there are issues with the actual text, they will suggest revisions, additions and deletions for any text that is repetitive or requires more detail to clarify it for readers. Structural editing involves a lot of back-and-forth communication between editor and author in order to address such issues as inadequate research, underdeveloped characterisation or unnecessary scenes.

When editing non-fiction manuscripts, a professional editor will assess your content to ensure the argument or purpose of the book is as clear and readable as possible. The editor will ensure that your text makes sense and is clearly worded and supported by sources that are verified. They will check to see that your word choices are suitable for your target audience in terms of age appropriateness and relevance, as well as ensuring that your style and tone match the subject matter. They may also advise you how you could rewrite some sections or chapters to improve the flow of your narrative, add new information for greater clarification, delete text that digresses from the main purpose of the book and reorganise content in a logical sequence to better connect chapters and sections so the manuscript reads as a cohesive whole.

When structurally editing a fiction manuscript, the editor will focus on the big-picture aspects of the story such as the narrative arc, characterisation, plot, point of view, dialogue and the purpose of the scenes. They will also focus on weeding out distractions from your core story, including characters who don't fit in well, settings that don't work, dialogue that adds nothing to the storyline, sub-plots that weaken the main plot, and digressions and non-productive elements that either dilute the essence of your story or actually detract from it. Fiction writing is a less formal mode of expression and authors are more at liberty to break grammar rules, so during the structural editing stage, an editor will usually pay less attention to the technicalities of language and more to the cohesive development of the storyline. In this way, an editor will focus on inconsistencies in a character's traits, dialogue weaknesses, and pacing and POV issues rather than polishing the actual language. As long as the story flows smoothly and the plot progresses easily from one scene to the next, specific language issues ultimately won't affect how the story is told.

Copyediting: crossing your 'T's and dotting your 'I's

While structural editing looks at the bigger picture perspective, the second editing stage – copyediting – consists of reviewing your manuscript at the sentence and word level. Copyediting (also referred to as 'line editing' or 'stylistic editing') is usually what people think of in relation to the word 'editing'. It involves checking your writing for any grammar, spelling, syntax and punctuation errors. But in addition to these vital language reviews, an editor will focus on the style, rhythm and flow of your writing, as well as its technical accuracy, consistency and clarity. They will delete any redundant words and phrases and add transitions between sentences and paragraphs in order to refine your style and tighten your prose. During this stage, an editor will also clarify any ambiguous phrasing or poorly constructed sentences.

While copyediting your manuscript, a professional editor will help you to fine-tune your language, as well as enhancing your unique style and voice. They will also ensure that there are no embarrassing errors or oversights in your text. Sometimes imperceptible details can make all the difference between a good and a great book. If you've written a fiction manuscript, have you ensured that each character stays true to their own personality and physical appearance throughout the story? Are your characters believable? Is their dialogue realistic? Have you unintentionally included conflicting descriptions of a scene? For example, you may have described the setting as 'a red brick home' on one page but 'a white weatherboard home' on a later page. Likewise, you may have inadvertently used both British–Australian English and American English spelling variations of a word interchangeably, such as 'colour' and 'color'. Here in Australia, the *Macquarie Dictionary* (8th edition at the time of writing) is regarded as the standard reference resource for Australian English. Throughout the writing process, you can consult this dictionary (which is also available online) to check the spelling of any words you are unsure about.

Finally, for non-fiction manuscripts, an editor will check any factual data (for example, confirming that all names, locations and dates are correct) during the copyediting process to ensure that it is accurate, as well as flagging any potential legal issues (such as defamation or copyright infringement) with the author. While editors are not lawyers, they are knowledgeable about certain publication laws that affect writers. I will be discussing this important issue in more detail in chapter 5.

Proofreading: checking it twice ... and then checking again!

Originally, proofreading referred to the late-stage correction of written content that had already been professionally set in lead type. Proofreading literally means 'reading and checking galley proofs' against the original document. These days, the term usually refers to the final checking process of any text-based material.

People often use the term 'proofreading' to refer to any kind of editing; however, in the world of book publishing, it involves the final quality control check after your edited Word manuscript has been typeset. This is not the time to make major changes to the text or to start rewriting. The purpose of proofreading is to identify any mistakes that may have slipped through the editing process, including spelling, punctuation, capitalisation, tense and inconsistencies with subject–verb agreement. A proofreader will also ensure that any formatting issues are dealt with, including errors in font size and styling, extra spaces between sentences, kerning and tracking issues (i.e. too much or too little word spacing and/or line spacing), widows (a single word on a line by itself) and orphans (a short or final line of a paragraph on the top of a page), as well as inaccuracies in running heads (the lines of text in the top margin) or page folios (i.e. page numbering). In this way, proofreading involves checking the formatted publication is typographically and grammatically correct and that it consistently conforms to any style decisions the editor applied during the copyediting process.

Proofreading is the last line of defence to check that an edited and formatted manuscript is as polished as possible before it is printed and released to the world. While a proofreader can't guarantee to catch every single typo or error, they will ensure that your published book is as close to error-free as humanly possible.

What's your style? Style guides to the rescue

Many of the guidelines relating to language usage that people regard as 'rules' are in fact style considerations, and they may not necessarily be consistent from one style guide to another. There are lots of different technical aspects of language that writers need to be aware of. Should you use a spaced en dash or an unspaced em dash in your text to set off an element added to amplify or digress from the main clause? How should titles and headings be formatted? While some of these questions are relatively easy to answer according to the rules of grammar, spelling and punctuation, other things are not so straightforward. This is because stylistic issues are often a matter of preference rather than being subject to strict rules, and they also change over time.

Writers need to have access to trusted resources that can resolve these issues, especially if they want to produce work that is both grammatically correct and stylistically consistent. This is where a style guide can come to your rescue. Editorial style guides (also sometimes referred to as style sheets) address common grammatical points and provide guidelines for formatting written content. They establish consistency in terms of spelling, punctuation, capitalisation, hyphenation and abbreviations, as well as the formatting of headings and the use of numbers. A style guide can save writers and editors from fretting over what is the 'right' style or format for a word or phrase and from wasting time searching for answers from a range of different reference sources.

Within academia, style guides also provide standards for citations, references and bibliographies. Many academic disciplines have their own style guides, such as the *Publication Manual of the American Psychological Association*, which is commonly used in social sciences and humanities. Likewise, many organisations create in-house style manuals in order to address the kinds of writing-related issues that are specific to them. Here in Australia, the online *Australian Government Style Manual* is considered the 'bible' for professional writers, editors, proofreaders, graphic designers and publishers, particularly those working in government and business areas. (In the United Kingdom, Oxford University Press's *New Oxford Style Manual* is a highly respected English language style guide, whereas in the United States, Strunk and White's *Elements of Style* and *The Chicago Manual of Style* are both widely used reference resources for style advice.)

Collaborating with a professional editor

As an author, I'm sure you're very aware of how much work goes into writing a book – numerous hours spent sitting in front of your computer screen, tapping away on your keyboard, and that's before you even begin to tackle the challenges involved in marketing your published book. So you might feel the need to try to save money by scrimping on certain publication steps, such as hiring a professional editor. This is not a good idea if you're planning to self-publish your book. We are all blind to our own writing and grammar mistakes: I wouldn't have considered publishing this book without first getting my manuscript professionally edited, and I'm an editor myself! Even though collaborating with an editor is a significant investment, both financially and emotionally, if you are keen to ensure your published manuscript is the best it can be, taking this route will end up paying dividends for your book many times over.

At the outset, it's important to consider an editor as your publication partner who has your best interests firmly in mind. Editing is a valuable investment in your book, as a professional editor can help transform your manuscript from 'okay' to 'awesome'! This is because an editor has a bird's-eye view of your text. They can see all the puzzle pieces and help you to assemble your content in a way that highlights your written words to best advantage. As a result, you can feel confident that readers will readily connect with your text from the very first page of your book to the last.

A professional editor will ensure that your final manuscript conveys a highly polished version of your written words and help you tell your story in the most engaging way possible. Nevertheless, many authors are shocked when they find out how much a professional editor's services will cost them. They may recognise that editors are highly educated professionals with a broad general knowledge (and possibly a particular subject expertise) and a specialised skill set and so deserve decent remuneration for their expertise; however, they still baulk at the quoted editing fee. But even though an editor's services might seem expensive, their expertise and guidance will probably save you a lot of time and embarrassment (and possibly also money) in the long run. Publishing an unedited book can be costly in terms of the potential harm to your reputation. Likewise, your book's sales will probably languish because readers usually avoid poorly written books that are riddled with errors.

These days, many editors are freelancers, which means they set their own rates and may charge per word, per hour or a set project package rate. But higher rates don't necessarily equate to the best editor; likewise, lower rates could actually turn out to be a waste of money. You should definitely take an

Chapter 4 – Your foundational editing checklist

editor's rates into consideration, but don't select someone based solely on price. If you do end up hiring a professional editor, you should budget on spending anywhere from five hundred to several thousand dollars (and sometimes even more) for a book-length manuscript.

If you have decided to invest in professional editing services for your book project, you should spend time researching online and considering various options before making your final decision. Aim to find an editor who you think will be a good fit for your book's genre or subject area. Check out the editor's website or LinkedIn profile to see what projects they have worked on and read testimonials from their previous clients. Next, consult with other writers (maybe you could ask around in your writers' group) to find out if anyone you know has worked with a good editor they can refer you to. Alternatively, you can research professional editing organisations online, including the Institute of Professional Editors (Australia and New Zealand), Chartered Institute of Editing and Proofreading (UK) and Editorial Freelancers Association (USA), and check out their searchable directories of editors. Reedsy and Upwork are two freelancing sites that are also potential options for sourcing editors and proofreaders (although it's important to note that the experience levels and skill sets of freelancers on these sites can vary from highly competent professionals to unqualified or unskilled workers).

Finally, many editors offer sample edits (either free or for a small sum), which is a great way for you to gain some insight into their particular editing style. This service can help you determine if an editor will be a good fit for your book project prior to committing to their full editing fee.

FIVE

Essential publishing issues to consider

While most writers focus on the creative or research aspects of producing a book, many underlying elements can influence how your book will resonate with your ideal readers. For example, a number of legal and ethical issues associated with book publication can have a significant impact on your future as an author. When you self-publish a book, you have a responsibility to ensure your content is acceptable from a legal, ethical and cultural perspective. You also want to ensure that your written words don't cause a backlash that will undermine all your hard work and put readers offside because you've offended them in some way. This will save you a lot of time and heartache further down the track. By developing your awareness of these issues from the outset, you can avoid having to spend hours rewriting your manuscript or even completely shelving the project. If you choose to ignore these crucial areas, your book might end up getting the 'thumbs down' from readers from the outset.

As an author, your ultimate goal should be to share your ideas or creative vision without harming anyone by inadvertently stealing their content, insulting their culture or offending them in some way. Most writers don't set out to do these things on purpose; however, if you are not aware of the risks, you can easily overlook inappropriate content in your text that could potentially come back to haunt you and ruin your reputation. Even fiction writing is bound by the need to represent facts and context in a way that is fair and reasonable. In other words, you cannot just say whatever you feel like and be immune from the consequences. While these legal and ethical concepts may seem intimidating, there's no need to feel daunted. By educating yourself about their importance, you can keep them in the back of your mind as you craft your story and shape the text within your manuscript.

Ideally, you want to write your manuscript in such a way that you are perceived as being reputable and trustworthy. This will permit you to be more successful in marketing your book and also if you are planning a sequel or another follow-up publishing project. If you publish content that is offensive and highly controversial, your work may receive a lot of attention; however, you could also find that your writing career is over before it has even begun. If you think about celebrities who have been the focus of a scandal, you probably don't want to find yourself in a similar situation. Even if there isn't a public backlash or a lawsuit, if a book doesn't 'feel' right, readers won't recommend it to their friends and other people (in person and via book review sites). And word-of-mouth is crucial in terms of marketing a product (in this case, your book).

Presenting authentic material will also cement your credibility with readers as you join the well-respected ranks of published authors. Overall, there is so much to be gained from observing legal and ethical considerations, and it will help to ensure a stress-free launch for your book. In the same way that you would try to protect yourself from other problems in life, you should think of these steps as being a form of insurance for your book project. After all your hard work writing and publishing your book, the anxiety of dealing with lawyers or coping with a public relations nightmare is the last thing you need.

So, let's move on to consider the major legal and ethical threats you need to be aware of as a self-publishing author. While they may seem overwhelming at first, by following this advice, you will be better equipped to avoid these potential risks to your reputation as a writer and possibly also your bank balance. You may also like to check out *The Australian Editing Handbook* (3rd edition) by Elizabeth Flann, Beryl Hill and Lan Wang for more information about ethical and legal aspects of book publishing.

Potential legal 'red flags' for authors

One of many advantages of self-publishing your book is that it offers you the ability to control the writing process and all the steps that follow. However, it also means that 'the buck stops with you', as you are responsible for ensuring your book does not violate any laws. You can easily circumvent potential problems by making some wise choices while you are drafting your manuscript. Every country has its own laws that apply to book publishing, but there are similar standards around the world. In the next few sections, we'll explore Australian laws that are relevant to publishing (including copyright and defamation) in more detail.

Copyright

If there is a quote or phrase from your favourite poem or song that you want to include in your book, you may think it is fair game because those words are well-known in the public sphere. However, this is an incorrect assumption. Your written content is protected by copyright law and so are other writers' texts. As an author, it is important for you to be aware of copyright law because it will help you to not only deal with other people's copyrighted material correctly, but also protect your own.

Copyright recognises and protects the intellectual property (IP) in a creative work, including written words, that someone produces. In Australia, the *Copyright Act 1968 (Cth)* automatically covers text, photos, illustrative artwork and music (among other forms of creative work) for the lifespan of the person who produced it plus 70 years after their death. (Depending on the type of creative work, there are some variations to this ruling, but this is the criteria that mostly applies to writers.) This means other people cannot copy, adapt, perform or publish your creative work (even online) without your written permission until 70 years after you die. Likewise, you cannot do the same thing to another writer's or artist's work.

Even when you paraphrase another writer's content, you may still need to obtain their written permission to use their IP for your own commercial gain. There are a couple of provisions within copyright law that may allow the use of someone else's work, but they are very specific. The best practice is to share the relevant passages with the original author and request their written permission to use them in your book.

Songwriters, in particular, are very protective of their creative content, and copyright laws reflect their desire to restrict free use of their lyrics in books. If you feel it is vital to include a quote from a song, the best option is to write to the musician to seek their permission. They will want to know the context of how their words will be used and could potentially charge you a hefty fee to grant permission to use their original content. So, for this reason, you might want to rethink including song lyrics in your book due to the associated costs and the delay involved while you apply for written permission.

In addition to written text, you need to ensure there are no copyright restrictions on any graphics (such as diagrams, graphs, charts and maps), photographs and illustrative artwork included in your book. You cannot just copy images from the internet and then use them in your book. Firstly, you need to find out whether an image is protected by copyright law or if it truly is in the public domain. Even if someone else has reproduced an image on their website, that does not excuse you from making the same error in judgement. Instead, you can purchase royalty-free images from stock image companies or download images from sites that offer public domain or Creative Commons content (as long as you closely follow their guidelines for giving the artist credit). For more helpful information and fact sheets about copyright, check out the Australian Copyright Council website.

Defamation

According to the Arts Law Centre of Australia, 'the law of defamation aims to balance the right of free speech in a community with the right to be protected from an attack on an individual's personal reputation in that community'.[2] Previously, defamation was divided into two categories, 'libel' and 'slander'. However, this distinction has become less important over time, and in 2006, uniform defamation legislation was introduced throughout Australia.

If you write something that could potentially cast someone in an unflattering light (whether you purposely meant to do so or not), you open yourself up to a defamation lawsuit. You

---

2. https://www.artslaw.com.au/information-sheet/defamation-law/

may think your comment was reasonable, but others may not view things in the same way. Defamation lawsuits are assessed in part on whether what you wrote contained a negative claim (referred to as an 'imputation'). The damages from these legal actions can range from a small sum to millions of dollars (depending on the perceived damage caused by the publication), plus the legal costs involved in defending yourself. So it's definitely a very good idea to steer clear of ending up in this situation in the first place!

To avoid any issues with defamation, it is important to make sure that your words don't have the potential to harm someone's reputation. Claiming that you were only repeating rumours or quotes made by other people, regardless of their truth, will not stand up in a court of law. Even if what you have written doesn't seem to you to be harmful at face value, it's possible that your text could imply to others something that's demeaning or damaging (i.e. a negative perception) about an individual or group of people or an organisation. If you are going to draw on truth and real-life characters for your book, you should avoid referring to anything that may be interpreted as having a negative impact on an individual's reputation or moral standing within the wider community.

Be careful about using judgemental wording when talking about characters, whether they are an individual or part of a specific group. You can easily describe people in a factual way without adding an extra layer of opinion that can be interpreted as being defamatory.

One possible defence against defamation is based on *proving* that what you published is largely true, so keep any documentation to back up your claims. Ensuring you are well prepared in order to avoid this legal minefield is your safest bet when self-publishing your book. More detailed information on the legal aspects of book publication is available from the Arts Law Centre of Australia. Similarly, anyone who is a member of the Australian Society of Authors can access low-cost publishing legal advice via Authors Legal. I also recommend that you seek advice from a professional lawyer to safeguard against any potential legal issues that might arise from your manuscript.

Ethical and cultural dilemmas ... and how to deal with them

As a writer, you are motivated by the story that you want to tell. While drafting your manuscript, you will likely draw from your own experience of the world around you or from your own imagination. But sometimes, aspects of your writing might unintentionally cause pain or distress to readers. Some people may be adversely affected by your book if the story you tell directly reflects them or their way of life. It is vital to be aware of, and sensitive to, social and cultural perspectives as a writer. Cultural differences are no excuse for you to criticise the lifestyles of other people. While staying as close as possible to the truth, you should avoid incorporating content in your book that could potentially hurt or offend other people.

This is an ethical boundary that writers should strive to stay within. Creativity loves to explore freely without restriction or restraint; however, this does not give you licence to inflict emotional pain on others. This could happen if your narrative portrays a certain gender, religion, cultural group or people of certain abilities or sexual orientation in a negative light.

> As an indie author, you don't have the backing of a traditional publisher with a legal team to check your manuscript for any potential signs of trouble. For this reason, you need to take some steps to educate yourself about this important aspect of book publishing. When you use your words to attack other people, you open yourself up to criticism and attack as well. The best way to prevent this from happening to you is to strive to be culturally aware and sensitive at all times.

A good way to avoid any potential ethical and cultural issues in your book is to work closely with a sensitivity reader. This person will have lived experience of the culture or background that is depicted in your book, so they will be able to inform you if your wording and descriptions are on the mark or not. This additional review does not replace the services of a professional editor or proofreader. A sensitivity reader can simply alert you to any stereotypes, offensive language or other gaps in cultural awareness that may be present in your manuscript. They will offer suggestions on how you can improve your text so it is more respectful. A sensitivity reader can help you to avoid any unintentional biases against, for example, someone from a specific country or culture, a member of the LGBTIQ+ community, or an individual living with a mental or physical disability.

We're all equal: using inclusive language

The world has become a global village. Walls of difference that previously separated us have now become connecting bridges to help us reach out and communicate with one another. The world you create in your manuscript should reflect the diversity of the world we live in today. Using outdated words and expressions that completely override or deny the rights of certain people indicates a lack of awareness and sensitivity on your part. Other people will find this practice offensive, and it also reflects poorly on your own character and integrity.

A generation ago, there were certain phrases you could have published without any fear of a negative reaction because the world had not yet progressed to our current level of consciousness of diversity and equality. These days, if you decide to incorporate old-fashioned idioms or stereotypes in your book and use them in the same context as they previously were, it is very likely that you will receive a backlash (and possibly there could also be legal ramifications). Your written text should respect the rights and opinions of every group within the community. Of course, acknowledging someone's opinion or belief does not necessarily mean that you agree with them. It simply signifies that you recognise their rights as individuals and that you expect the same treatment from them in return.

Language is evolving all the time, so it's important to stay up-to-date as the culture around us changes and evolves. This means using words that people would use to describe themselves, rather than referencing past labels or lumping certain groups together. For example, describing someone as 'non-white' tells readers who they are not, rather than who they are. Specifically, you should avoid using language that is recognised as being sexist, racist or judgemental in any way. It is not necessary to express yourself this way in order to get your point across. Using racist labels or derogatory words that malign someone based on their physical/mental abilities or sexual orientation is disrespectful and will attract negative attention to your narrative. Having said that, for fiction writing, you do have some artistic licence with regard to the language and behaviour of your characters (especially your antagonist). However, you should ensure you can justify this tactic as being essential to your story's plot and characterisation.

For more information about the use of inclusive language, I recommend you refer to such resources as the *Australian Government Style Manual* or the *Chicago Manual of Style*. For gender issues, the *Conscious Style Guide* and *GLAAD Media Reference Guide* are helpful resources, while for disability issues, the *Disability Language Style Guide* and *People With Disabilities Australia (PWDA) Language Guide* provide valuable guidance. You can also learn more from online forums and by consulting someone within the particular community you mention in your writing.

Although you may be writing your book for a specific group of people who agree with you rather than for the entire world, as I mentioned previously, the world has become a global village. For this reason, it is important to balance your opinions with other people's feelings and sensitivities. Always keep in mind that your book is meant to engage, educate and/or entertain your reader. The last thing you want to do is to enrage them and give them a reason to put your book down. While this is important from a legal standpoint, it's also simply a case of treating people with respect and common courtesy.

Citing references in your book

If you have written a non-fiction manuscript, citing any other reference resources you consulted to create your written work is an essential task. For the most part, if the ideas in your book draw on content that has been produced by other people, it's important to give credit to the other writers who have informed or inspired you. If you conducted your own research, you need to outline your processes and the contributions of any other people who helped you. The purpose of citing references is credibility and integrity. It also demonstrates that you are committed to providing quality content to your audience, while at the same time respecting another creative's moral rights.

Once you have collated all the relevant references you used to write your manuscript, you need to arrange this information in a consistent citation format. There are different ways to do this, but two well-known systems are the Harvard referencing style and the American Psychological Association (often referred to as 'APA') referencing style. As you progressively write your book manuscript, the simplest approach is to add any references you have consulted to a list. Going back to do this task later is not only tedious but also means that you may overlook some resources.

With all these issues, being respectful of other writers and your reading audience should be your guiding light. If you feel as though you're treading too close to a legal or ethical line, you should trust your instincts and adapt your wording accordingly. While there are obviously costs involved, you may also like to consider asking a lawyer who specialises in publishing to review your work, or just certain passages, so you feel reassured that you are on firm legal ground. It could save you additional expense, stress and delays later on in the publication process.

SIX

Getting the structure right for your book

Having spent countless hours writing your manuscript, no doubt you are keen for your final published book to be on par with any book you'd buy from a bookshop. This is where having a basic understanding of book publishing (including book composition and structure) can help you to successfully achieve this outcome. Ensuring your manuscript is structured properly so that your book has a professional look and feel will mean that readers, reviewers and book buyers will take your content seriously.

The way in which you structure your book acts as the bait that will hook readers into your narrative. An effective analogy to demonstrate this point is to consider that a book should be structured similarly to a movie. A movie generally doesn't commence with a long list of people who were involved in its production. Instead, the director will begin the film with a beautiful scenery shot or a dramatic or intriguing background that sets the tone for the rest of the movie. Some production companies will even skip that initial scene-setting step altogether and start out with a high-tension dramatic action sequence that causes viewers to grip their seats in excitement.

This dramatic scene will then play out for a brief period before seguing into the introductory credits, followed by the main storyline, and then the names of all the people who were involved in the production are scrolled on screen at the end.

The format typically used for the narrative structure of a mainstream movie focuses on capturing the viewers' attention so they become invested in the storyline the scriptwriter and director want to tell them. While writing your manuscript, it can be helpful to keep this same technique in mind for the structure of your book. Reflect on what information you want your readers to see first and how that might have an impact on their emotional connection to your writing. If you consider this scenario from a completely visual angle, a published book does not usually have the same degree of creative freedom that movies have. However, there are certain similar elements you can use when creating the structure of your book that will help ensure your reader becomes invested in your written content.

In this chapter, we'll explore the typical structure of a book (particularly non-fiction). We'll also consider how you can determine which structure is suitable for your book according to its genre or subject area. And if you are interested in learning more about this topic, I highly recommend Joel Friedlander's excellent publication, *The Book Blueprint: Expert Advice for Creating Industry-Standard Print Books*.

Everything in its correct place: typical structural elements of a book

Ultimately, the way in which you decide to structure your book largely depends on whether you have written a non-fiction manuscript to share your expertise or interest in a factual topic or whether you want to share your creativity in the form of a novel or series of short stories. In this chapter I will primarily

Chapter 6 – Getting the structure right for your book

focus on the typical elements of a non-fiction manuscript, because structuring a novel is an in-depth subject that warrants an entire separate book to do it justice.

While non-fiction books should aim to stay as close to the facts as possible, writing a non-fiction manuscript still involves creative input to achieve the best outcome. In fact, as a non-fiction author, it's crucial that you organise the information contained in your book in the most visually appealing and engaging way possible for your readers.

Generally speaking, non-fiction books are organised into to the following three distinct parts, each with their own purpose and sub-divisions:

1. *Front matter* – the pages at the beginning of the book; includes book administration (i.e. ISBN), author, publisher, printing company and copyright information.
2. *Body* – the main written content of the book, usually arranged in chapters and/or parts.
3. *Back matter* – the pages at the back of the book, containing reference lists, notes and other supplemental material.

The front matter includes a variety of pages and sections that display all the different parts of a book. These typically include a title page, copyright page (containing copyright notice and library cataloguing information), table of contents, acknowledgements and/or dedication, foreword, preface and/or introduction. The pages in the front matter are usually numbered using lower-case roman numerals. The reason for this is so the remainder of the book does not have to be renumbered if other preliminary pages (such as a dedication) are added after the book has been finalised for printing.

The largest and most important part is the actual body content of the book, and this material is usually arranged into chapters (in both non-fiction and fiction manuscripts). For non-fiction books that contain a large amount of written content, this material is often also divided into separate parts. Similarly, fiction books may also include a prologue at the front which offers readers an initial hint about the storyline and/or an epilogue which ties up any loose ends at the end of the book.

A book's back matter might incorporate an afterword, appendix, glossary, bibliography and/or index. These items can be helpful in bringing closure or providing additional information for readers.

Copyright/imprint page: signalling ownership of your creative content

The copyright page (which is also referred to as the 'imprint page') is positioned on the back of the title page in the front matter of a book. The purpose of the copyright page is to indicate that you have ownership over the content in your book. This signals that your written content isn't in the public domain but, rather, that it is your IP and cannot be copied without your permission. The copyright page also usually contains data that is helpful for distributors, librarians and book retailers, including edition and/or printing information, cataloguing statement, legal disclaimers and the book's ISBN details.

> Technically speaking, you don't actually require a special page to indicate you are the copyright owner of your manuscript, as it is considered your IP as soon as you've written it. However, if you don't include a copyright page in your book, your IP could potentially be harder to prove in a court of law.

Acknowledgements and dedications: thanking the key people

The acknowledgement and/or dedication section is your opportunity to express your gratitude to the people who have helped you to publish your book. If you take time to reflect over your life and the steps involved in shaping you into the person you are today, no doubt there are some key people who have supported you on your path. Whatever role these people have played, the acknowledgement or dedication page is an opportunity for you to recognise them and thank them for their help. The book you are writing will be a lasting legacy you'll leave behind. So what better way to show your appreciation to the people who have contributed to that legacy than by allocating a special page in your book to communicate your thanks?

Keep your 'thank you' message short and sweet. Your text should be simple, uncomplicated and to the point. Stick to the basic facts, ensure your message is sincere and heartfelt, and then move on to the main content of your book.

Foreword, preface and introduction: what's the difference?

It is important to understand the difference between these three publication elements so you can decide how to best use them in your book.

Foreword

The foreword in a book is written by someone other than the author. It could be a celebrity, a well-known author who writes in the same genre, or someone who is considered to be an expert in the subject area of the book. The purpose of the foreword is to give credibility to the book and endorse its author.

In other words, the foreword tells the reader why they should trust the content within the book by leveraging the reputation of the person who has written this section.

Preface

A preface is written by the author and addressed to the reader directly. In the preface, you usually share what motivated you to write your book in the first place. Were you inspired by a particular incident? What are the major themes? What do you hope people will gain from reading your book? The language you use here should be simple and relatable. That way, the reader understands that you have personally experienced what you are going to be discussing in the body of your book.

Introduction

The introduction focuses on the content of the book. As the name implies, its purpose is to introduce your readers to the structure and scope of your manuscript. Within this section, you can state the goals and purpose of the main body of your book. You might also want to explain certain aspects of the text that you think people need to understand before they commence reading. In this way, the introduction serves as a guide as to why your book answers your readers' questions and how it offers solutions to their problems.

The final curtain: conclusion, appendices, glossary, bibliography, index

Unlike a movie where the viewer can be left hanging in limbo, a book should create closure for the reader. This is where all the structural elements listed below play a part in tying up any loose ends in the book.

Conclusion

The conclusion essentially involves wrapping everything you have discussed in the main body of your book into a tight bow. In this section you offer the reader encouragement and support, as well as expressing your hope that the message you have shared in the text has had a positive impact on them. A well-written conclusion can create a bonding experience between you and your readers, particularly if you have written a self-help book. It can make your reader feel as though you 'have their back' and understand their problems and pain points.

Appendices

An appendix usually provides supplementary information to the main content of a book. It is placed at the back of the book for readers to use as a reference resource or to expand on the topics covered in the body text in more detail.

Glossary

A glossary is like a mini-dictionary – it contains a list of specific words used in the book that may be unfamiliar to readers. For instance, if you have written a fantasy book set in an imaginary world or you are writing about a niche topic that uses certain terminologies people may be unaware of, the glossary is the perfect place for you to explain these concepts to your reader.

Bibliography

A bibliography (also referred to as a list of references or resources) is an itemised list of books, articles, websites and other sources that you have consulted during the writing process for your book. It provides credibility to your non-fiction (or, occasionally, fiction) book by signalling that you didn't just pluck the information in your manuscript out of thin air. Likewise, it gives readers a good place to start if they want to do their own research on the topic. While a bibliography is often organised alphabetically, it can also be arranged by theme, topic or order of appearance.

Index

If you have written any type of reference book (including cookbooks), you may wish to incorporate an index at the back. An index is an alphabetised list of terms that includes the page number or links to these words in the main body of the book. It is similar to a dictionary; however, its main purpose is to serve as a reference tool rather than to define specific words. The index should be the very last step in the publication process for your book. You should delay creating an index until after the typesetting and proofreading stages have been finalised, since any revisions to the text could affect the index page numbering or links.

Entice your audience: back cover blurb and author bio

While, strictly speaking, the blurb and author bio aren't usually considered to be parts of a book's structure, I've included these two elements here as they are important marketing tools. A well-written blurb and a thoughtfully crafted bio are designed to entice readers to purchase your book. Obviously, the front cover is the main feature to attract readers' attention and encourage them to take a closer look at your book. When they do stop scrolling through an online store or pick up a copy of your book in a bookshop, the blurb (and to a lesser extent your author bio) can help to convince them to buy it.

In succinct terms, a 'blurb' is a short description that is meant to act as promotional copy for your book. The purpose of the blurb is to convert a browsing reader into a paid customer.

Chapter 6 – Getting the structure right for your book

Typically, there are two types of blurbs: descriptive blurbs and review blurbs. A descriptive blurb is incorporated on the back cover of a book, while a review blurb is usually featured on websites or online sales platforms such as Amazon or Book Depository to promote the book. For our purposes, I'll focus on descriptive blurbs and how you can create an effective piece of text that will help you market your book.

The following tips can help you to draft an effective blurb for your book.

- It needs to be short and catchy; this is not the time to launch into a long spiel about the storyline or the inspiration behind your book. Try to restrict this text to a maximum of 250 words.
- It should have an attention-grabbing headline or tagline.
- It should include details such as the book's genre and main theme. Introducing the main protagonist and creating some mystery around the main storyline conflict is an excellent tactic to use for fiction books.
- The final sentence should spark the reader's curiosity. A common strategy is to use a question that's designed to hook the reader in so they want to discover the answer by buying and reading your book.

In contrast, the author bio offers a sneak peek into the person who has written the book (which in this case is you!). Written from the third-person perspective, both the 'About the author' section within the book and the shorter author bio on the back cover present information about the writer that readers might find interesting. The average length of an author bio usually varies between 75 and 200 words. Your bio can be written in a serious manner to establish your credibility in your particular subject area, or it can be quirky or humorous in order to connect emotionally with your readers. If you are concerned about privacy, your author bio does not have to go into an in-depth description or contain very personal details. All it needs to do is provide some basic information that will give readers an insight into you as a person.

* * *

So far we've considered how to get your thoughts onto the page and then polish your writing to present your story or message in the best possible light. In part three, we'll progress from finessing your written words to focusing on the design and administrative stages of the book publishing process.

PART THREE

The Perfect Package For Your Narrative

SEVEN

Between the covers: your book's internal design

A book's cover is designed to attract readers, but the internal page design is what will keep them committed to its content. And like your book's cover, the internal pages should be well-designed. While the format of the internal pages isn't usually as elaborate or complex as the cover design, it is a key aspect to ensuring your book's success in the marketplace. People may go to a bookshop, pick up a book with an eye-catching cover, open it up at any page, only to decide that the text font is too small or the words are too cramped for them to want to read the book, even if they're interested in its subject area or genre. A well-designed internal page layout is visually appealing and allows the book's content to be easily comprehended. In the same way that engaging the services of a professional architect will result in a well-built house, focusing on the various design elements of your book's internal pages will ensure a high-quality outcome.

The page layout design of a book should suit its content. For example, the page layout for a novel or memoir should permit the reader to progress steadily through the book and become fully immersed in the narrative without any distractions, such as an overly elaborate font style or decorative images. Textbooks, travel guides, coffee-table books and cookbooks usually contain numerous graphic elements such as photographs, diagrams, charts, textboxes and tables, so their internal page formatting is often more complex and specialised than text-only books.

In this chapter, I will discuss the interior page layout design of books and why this is such an important aspect of the publication process. While it is possible to format the internal pages of your book yourself in Microsoft Word, I highly recommend that you work with a professional typesetter. Using Adobe InDesign (which is industry-standard desktop publishing software), typesetters are able to precisely format your book's internal page layout to create a professional-looking outcome that satisfies printing specifications, including correct trim size, embedded fonts and proper colour profile for images (i.e. CMYK, not RGB). Regardless of which route you opt for, if you'd like to learn more about this fascinating area of book design, check out *The Design Manual* by David Whitbread.

The optimal medium for your message

Written text is often not the only element that appears on the pages of a book, although it may be for most novels and many narrative-style non-fiction books. Graphic elements such as photos, illustrations, diagrams, charts, graphs and tables can also enhance your book. When opting whether to use text only or text and images in your book, keep your readers – and how to effectively communicate your message to them – firmly in mind. Your final decision about your book's page layout design should be influenced by its content and what you think will deliver an enjoyable reading experience for your target audience.

Chapter 7 – Between the covers: your book's internal design

If you believe that your written words on their own will be appealing to your readers, then opt for that approach. For example, a simple and straightforward text-only layout design works well for novels and collections of short stories. However, if you feel your book's text needs to be supplemented with images, you should take that route instead. For example, if you have written a fantasy novel set in an imaginary world, including a map can be a useful visual aid for readers. This illustrative artwork will provide a visual indication of the setting for your story and increase your book's aesthetic appeal. Many non-fiction authors use images to enhance their message to readers. For instance, a biography about a famous person typically contains written text with photographic insert sections. Likewise, many cookbooks consist of complex layout designs with step-by-step instructional text for recipes, accompanied by multiple photographs and other graphics.

For books that contain a mix of text and images, the internal page layout design should be formatted to showcase all the elements to best advantage. Ensure the images have sufficient negative space within the book's layout design to 'breathe'; one carefully positioned image can often be more effective than a collage of many. Depending on the genre of your book, the text and images need to interact in unison and suit the audience demographic. For example, children's picture books usually include a very small amount of text on each page as the illustrative artwork is the major component of the layout design. A coffee-table style photography book might contain large glossy photos on each page, with simple captions under each image and a brief text introduction at the front. Both text and images within your book's page layout design should be formatted to allow readers to readily engage with your content.

Major influences on book layout design

While you may have your own ideas, your book's target reading audience and its genre or subject area are majors influences in determining the layout design of the internal pages of your book.

Target audience for your book

When researching your ideal readers and how to target your book to them, you should think carefully about the message you might be subconsciously conveying about its content via the page layout design. At the end of the day, your target readers are the people you want your published book to most appeal to because they might buy it. However, the decision-making processes associated with book buying can be more complex and involve more participants than just your end reader. As well as the intended (or 'primary') reading audience, there may also be a secondary audience (e.g. a gift-giver buying a coffee-table travel book or a cookbook as a present for someone) that is actively involved in book-purchasing decisions, so it's important that your manuscript also entices them.

This scenario is particularly relevant for children's books, which are ultimately intended for our mini-readers. However, the person who decides to purchase a children's book is not usually the child: it's their parents (or other adults such as grandparents and other relations) who select a book they think the child will enjoy, often based on its page layout format (as well as associated design elements like the cover design).

Genre or subject area of your book

The genre of your book can influence whether you should use more graphics and less text (or vice versa). When browsing in a bookshop, a lot of book buyers quickly flip through the pages of a book just to get a sense of its actual content and genre. For example, if the subject area of your coffee-table book is home interior design, it makes sense to include high-quality photographs, not only because they will enhance readers' enjoyment of your content but because that's what readers have come to expect from a coffee-table book on interior design.

And it's not just readers' purchasing decisions you need to be concerned about; you also want them to be able to readily engage with your book's content. However, you will make that task more challenging for readers if your book's internal design doesn't adhere to the usual page formatting conventions for your specific genre. For example, the objective of most non-fiction books is to solve a problem for an individual reader or an organisation. Consequently, the internal page design of the book should effectively communicate the author's informational solution, which can be achieved by using graphics such as diagrams, charts, tables and illustrations to complement the text.

Consider whether readers will be less likely to understand your meaning if your book doesn't contain any graphics. Remember, people have very short attention spans these days and tend to skim-read for information. For this reason, creating a text-heavy book that involves reading for extended periods of time could deter some people from buying your book.

> If you are finding it difficult to figure out exactly how you'd like the internal pages of your book to be formatted, I suggest you spend time researching books in the same or a similar genre or subject area as yours. Pay attention to how the text and/or graphic content is laid out within them. But don't just stop there – investigate online to find out how popular these books are, as this will offer you some insight into whether their page layout design was appealing to readers or not.

Fundamental elements of internal page formatting

Formatting the internal pages of a book involves much more than selecting a nice font, typesetting the text and positioning any associated graphics within the page layout design. It also requires paying attention to the page trim size, margins, spacing between elements on each page, text alignment and heading hierarchy, as well as the finer details of the front and back matter (including page folios). In this way, the internal page structure should give readers a visual break between each segment of a book which, in turn, with help them to stay engaged with your narrative.

Below are some important factors with regards to the internal page layout of books.

Typeface selection

As a general rule of thumb, you should limit the number of typefaces used in your book to two or three. This will help to ensure that your book has a more consistent and coherent look and feel. For fiction books, using a single typeface will ensure that you don't 'break the spell' for readers by adding unnecessary distractions to your book's text. However, if you have written a non-fiction manuscript that incorporates a few heading levels, it can be a good idea to use two (or sometimes three) different typefaces so they stand out and make the content more visually engaging.

Text alignment

Text alignment relates to the way the written content in a paragraph is arranged in relation to the margins, including left aligned, right aligned, centred and justified. Careful consideration should be given to how the written text is formatted during the typesetting process to ensure it is visually appealing and free from distractions for readers. Designing paragraphs so they are easier for people's eyes to skim over can also produce a more pleasurable reading experience. Above all, it is important to avoid using multiple text alignment settings, as this will make your book's text look messy and unprofessional.

Margins and negative space

Page layout elements such as margins and negative space (which is also referred to as 'white space') are important aspects of internal page design of books, and their prime function is to improve readability of the text. There are three main margins within the page layout grid: the outside edge, the top edge and the bottom edge of the page. In addition, there is an inside margin (or 'gutter') where the pages of a book are bound together either by glue, staples or some type of spiral binding. The depth of both the top and the bottom margins influences where the running heads and feet (i.e. information such as book title, author name or chapter headings, along with page folios) should be positioned.

A well-designed internal page layout will incorporate plenty of negative space to balance the text and images contained in the book. Books with more pages cost more money to print, so some authors think it is a good idea to try to squeeze as much text (plus images if relevant) as possible onto a page. While you may be able to save a little bit by doing this, the visual appeal and readability of your book will suffer. A lack of negative space will produce a tight page layout and your content will look crowded, which, in turn, results in an unpleasant reading experience.

Heading level hierarchy

Headings act as signposts to help readers navigate their way through a book. Headings and subheadings provide information about a book's organisational structure, as well as offering a clear roadmap for readers so they can identify their current location within the text. For this reason, the various heading levels (level 1, level 2, level 3 etc) in a book need to be formatted consistently, and the 'emphasis' typographical elements (such as variations in typeface style, type size, bolding and/or italics) should reinforce the hierarchy structure. This is particularly relevant for non-fiction rather than fiction, as people often 'dip into' and skim through these types of books rather than reading them sequentially from front to back cover.

Chapter and section breaks

The purpose of chapter and section breaks is to prevent the text from appearing cluttered and to ensure the content in your manuscript is well structured. Chunking text into chapters and sections makes it more manageable for your readers and helps to ensure they remain engaged with your narrative. Chapter and section breaks are like milestones that allow readers to take a mental 'rest' to digest the ideas and/or storyline in your book.

These are a few basic elements associated with the page layout design of books (some of which I have incorporated within this book). In the remainder of this chapter, we'll explore other textual and graphic elements that influence the appearance of a book's internal pages.

Which typefaces work best?

A major decision associated with the internal page design of a book involves choosing a specific typeface or font. There are many typefaces available, but not all of them are appropriate for book design. If you want people to enjoy reading your book, it's important to select the right typeface, because the typeface you use conveys a message about the tone and style of your written content. In addition, there are other considerations

Chapter 7 – Between the covers: your book's internal design

(such as readability or legibility) that need to be taken into account with typeface selection.

So how then do you decide which typeface(s) to use? Typefaces can be grouped into two broad categories: serif and sans serif. A serif is a stroke that adds stems or 'feet' to the ends of a letter. Serif typefaces are commonly used as an industry standard for publishing books. This typeface style is often used for the body text, as the smooth curves of the letters make it easier for the eye to follow. Examples of popular serif typefaces used for text in books include Garamond Pro, Caslon Pro, Bembo and Sabon.

In contrast, a sans serif typeface has no stroke to finish off the edges of the letters. This typeface style is usually harder to read in books (such as novels and memoirs) that contain a lot of text. Sans serif typefaces have a more contemporary look and work well for headings, as well as in children's books. Other styles such as script typefaces, decorative typefaces and handwritten typefaces are not suitable for large amounts of body text but can be used for cover text or special ornamental features. To help simplify the typeface selection process for your book, I've provided some tips below to get you started.

Opt for legibility

Your readers should be able to consume your book's content without having to strain their eyes. While certain typefaces look very attractive, they can become distracting if they are used for a large amount of text. This, in turn, will detract from the message you want to communicate to your readers. Ultimately, the font style and size of the text in your book should be appropriate for your ideal readers. For example, the text in a children's picture book requires a larger-sized font than that used in a collection of academic articles.

Consider line spacing and length

There should be sufficient space (referred to as 'leading') between the lines of text on a page to help readers readily comprehend your message. If your text is tightly jammed together, people will find it hard to read and it will be challenging for them to absorb your content. As a general rule, you should stick to a maximum of 33 to 36 lines of text per page.

Line length is another characteristic you need to consider for the internal pages of your book. It's important to strike a balance between the length of lines of text on a page to ensure they are not too short or too long. Lines of text that are too long make it difficult for readers to focus on the actual content. Similarly, lines of text that are too short are challenging because the reader's eyes are forced to travel back to the start of the next line more often, thereby creating a break in their natural reading rhythm.

Finally, if your sentences are clustered together in long paragraphs without any line breaks, people will subconsciously feel tired even before they begin reading your text. Ensure all the paragraphs in the body text are clearly delineated by using either an indented or a block spacing style. Just remember, you shouldn't use both paragraph styles at once within your book!

Resolution is key: the benefits of high-resolution images

There is a common expression that a picture is worth a thousand words, and many authors would agree with this. The images you include in your book can help you tell your story even before your reader has finished the first sentence. An intriguing image can spark the curiosity of readers. However, if you use lacklustre or low-quality images, the perception you are projecting to readers is that your book's content is equally uninspiring and unprofessional. Even if an image looks okay on your computer screen, there's no guarantee that it will reproduce well in your published book. In particular, low-resolution images will appear pixelated and of poor quality when printed on paper stock. The two largest international on-demand printers (Amazon's Kindle Direct Publishing and IngramSpark) stipulate that all images within a book should have a minimum resolution of 300 dpi where possible, so you should assume that any images which have a lower resolution may not be suitable for your printed book.

If you want your published book to contain full-page and/or double-page colour 'spreads' of images, your image files need to be a very high resolution. High-resolution files will produce a detailed reproduction of the image at the desired size in printed format. In contrast, if you try to enlarge a low-resolution image file, it may end up looking pixelated and blurry in your final printed book.

Respecting other creatives' IP

In the same way that your written text conveys your knowledge or imaginative ideas to your audience, images are a unique artistic expression by their creator. Consequently, images (including photographs, illustrations and other original design artwork) are protected by some form of copyright legislation in most countries. Unless otherwise stated, it is important to consider all images as being in copyright. As previously discussed in chapter 5, using copyright images from the internet or from other published sources is actually stealing someone's IP. This means that you could potentially be sued for infringing their copyright. In order to use copyrighted images in your book, you need to seek written permission from the copyright owner, who may or may not allow you to use their image for free.

So what can you do if you're not a photographer, illustrator or artist yourself and you want to include images in your book? Possible options include:

- sourcing public domain images
- hiring a professional to create original image artwork for you
- purchasing royalty-free high-resolution images from an online stock image library.

Most images that are in the public domain have been organised within collections that use the Creative Commons 0 licence. This is not a formal legal licence but, rather, a convenient way of permitting anyone to use these images for their personal purposes. Commissioning a photographer, illustrator or graphic designer to create customised artwork for you is another alternative you could consider; however, this option is often expensive and time-consuming.

In contrast, sourcing high-resolution images from a stock image library can be a great way of finding the perfect photograph or illustration for your book at a reasonable cost. The main advantage of using royalty-free stock images (which includes photographs, illustrations and vector artwork) is the associated savings in time and money, as they have already been created and, hence, are ready for immediate use. As soon as you pay for a royalty-free photograph or illustration in a stock image library, you can download the high-resolution JPG or EPS file. One important point to note here is that when you buy an image from a stock image library, you're only purchasing a *licence to use* the image. The photographer or illustrator still owns the copyright for their image; you are simply paying for the right to use it within certain accepted terms.

* * *

Chapter 7 – Between the covers: your book's internal design

In the next chapter, I'll discuss the process of designing a cover for your book. At this point, I recommend you commission a professional cover designer for this important task. I know it can appear as though you have to spend more money than you'd ideally like to, particularly if you've already got a definite idea of what you want for your book's cover. However, in the long run, this investment will pay dividends for you as author. Like any other profession, book design requires extensive knowledge and experience to produce a good outcome. Once again, the house building analogy is useful here – a home renovation project that has been done by a professional building contractor always looks better than a DIY job.

EIGHT

Judging a book by its cover

No doubt you're familiar with the joke about people who won't read a book that doesn't contain any images; the thought of reading a book that mostly contains text is very off-putting (or even intimidating) for some people. Well, the truth is that even fewer people are willing to read a book that doesn't have an interesting or attractive cover design.

It's widely acknowledged that people will (pre)judge your book by its cover. Therefore, it makes good sense to ensure the design you use on the cover of your book is attention-grabbing at first glance. This is because you won't get a second chance to entice readers ... unless you happen to have a bunch of loyal fans who are willing to read your book regardless of what's on the cover. Anything less is probably going to leave your book gathering dust on a shelf for a very long time. The goal of an effective cover design is to attract readers so they are motivated to pick *your* book up from a shelf in a bookshop or select it from an online store in order to discover what's inside. If you're fishing for readers, your book's cover is a powerful hook.

The main purpose of a book cover is not to tell the story or to reveal its content; it's the first step (and arguably the most important aspect) in marketing a book. According to a survey conducted in 2010 by *The Book Smugglers*, a popular book-reviewing blog, 40% of respondents agreed when asked, 'Has a cover ever been the sole driving factor in your decision to purchase a book?'[3] Even if your content is phenomenal, if you want your book to sell well (and be read by people other than your family and friends!), the cover must have an eye-catching design. And in order to achieve the best outcome, you should work with a professional designer – someone who has extensive knowledge and experience in this space. Think of your book's cover design as a marketing investment, not just another item to tick off your list of things to do to get your book out into the world. A professional-looking cover will attract your ideal readers, while a bad cover can seriously harm its sales.

Obviously, the imagery that appears on the front cover is all-important, and it's the aspect of the book cover design authors tend to focus on. But while selecting a striking 'hero' image is vital to capturing readers' attention, the choice of appropriate typeface for the text elements on the cover (i.e. book title, subtitle if relevant and author name) is also significant. In other words, you can't just place any typeface next to an image and expect they will work well in unison. Certain design principles and aesthetics need to be taken into account.

We won't delve into these principles in detail here, as this topic alone would fill an entire book. Instead, our focus will be on how you can effectively communicate the aesthetic you envision for your book's cover to a professional designer. This is important, because designers aren't mind-readers. Also, it is quite likely that they won't allocate time to read your book's entire narrative prior to creating your cover design. So you need to be able to clearly explain your design concept to ensure they

---

3. https://www.thebooksmugglers.com/2010/04/cover-matters-the-survey-results.html

accurately interpret your vision and use their creative abilities to (hopefully) meet or exceed your expectations.

But before we explore how you can collaborate with a book designer, let's first consider the anatomy of a book cover, as well as the impact that genre or subject area has on creating a cover design that will be successful in the marketplace.

Anatomy of a book cover

A book cover has two key parts: the front cover and the back cover. Connecting the front and back covers is the book's 'spine'. The width of a book spine is determined by the total number of pages, the binding style and the thickness of the paper stock used. In the case of 'perfect-bound' paperbacks, the spine is the slim part of the book's outer shell where the internal pages are glued to the cover. For books with 'saddle-stitched' binding or spiral or comb binding, the spine is not an intrinsic aspect of the cover design artwork, whereas for hard-back (casebound) books, the spine is a much more distinctive feature. Typically, if you commission a professional designer to create your book's cover design, they will be responsible for creating the entire cover artwork – front, spine and back. This is the best approach, as it ensures there is design consistency between the different parts of the book cover.

A professional-looking book cover design should contain a definite hierarchy of design elements so that prospective readers can immediately tell:

- the title
- the author's name
- the genre (e.g. non-fiction or fiction)
- what the book is about.

All this information needs to be communicated by the cover design to someone who might only glance at it for a few seconds. A good book designer will be aware of how each element best fits within the cover design hierarchy and also understand the reason why.

In an effort to reduce costs, some authors decide to only get a front cover designed for their book. This is alright if you want your book to be available in ebook format only. However, if you want to publish printed copies of your book, then you will require a full book cover laid out in accordance with the correct trim size dimensions and exported as a press-ready PDF file. Since it's very easy to produce an ebook cover from the full cover, it makes sense to create the entire book cover design at the outset.

Fitting in versus standing out

As creatives, many of us struggle with this concept. We want to be recognised as individuals with unique abilities, so we naturally want our book's cover design to be incomparable; we don't want it to just fit in with the 'rest of the crowd'. We think that people will be able to immediately identify our book from the vast sea of books available for sale. But here's the thing: when you focus too much on standing out, you miss out on the opportunity for your book to gain traction in the marketplace.

What do I mean by this?

People tend to gravitate towards the familiar. The more familiar something (or someone) is, the more likely it is that others will be attracted to it. This is because we prefer things we know and can easily categorise. When we are searching for a new book to read, we want to feel reassured that it will be similar to the type of books we're used to and already enjoy. In his book, *The Author's Guide to Cover Design*, book cover

Chapter 8 – Judging a book by its cover

designer Stuart Bache refers to this concept as 'Familiarity Theory'. He recommends authors think of their book's cover as marketing packaging rather than a piece of unique artwork. According to Stuart, 'playing it safe' (yet still ensuring your book's cover is professional-looking) is preferable to attempting to produce a wildly unique design.

Making decisions is tiring as it involves a lot of cognitive input. For this reason, we constantly search for ways to shortcut this process ... and that includes anything that helps us decide what we should read next. The cover design of a book should offer subtle clues that subliminally signal a message to readers so they will be automatically drawn to it. Genres have conventions or reader expectations, much like tropes. Ideally, readers should be able to immediately recognise the genre of a book when they first glance at its cover. If people can connect your book to a specific genre without having to read a single word of the text, they might subconsciously decide that they like it and, in turn, buy a copy. This concept is particularly relevant to fiction versus non-fiction book covers. People who enjoy reading fiction are looking for a pleasurable escape from their daily lives and often don't respond to the realistic design style of many non-fiction book covers ... and vice versa.

An effective cover design needs to tell its own story and make a promise to the reader about the content of the book. In the case of fiction books, the purpose of the cover is to convey mood, emotion and ambience rather than being an exact replica of a scene or characters from the story. Readers expect to get a sneak peek of the action they're about to experience or to feel emotionally connected to the main protagonist. Science fiction, thriller/horror, fantasy and mystery cover designs tend to use darker imagery or scenes that create an atmosphere of intrigue or other-worldliness. Romance, chick-lit and religious/

spiritual covers usually lean more towards lighter colours and softer imagery. For non-fiction books, the cover design should connect with readers on both an emotional and intellectual level. Non-fiction books set out to solve a problem, so the imagery on the cover should signal to readers that the author will be offering them a solution.

A prudent investment: working with a professional designer

Unless you've decided to completely head down the DIY path, you're probably already aware that it's not a good idea for you to design your book's cover yourself using Microsoft Word (or even Microsoft Publisher). A professional-looking book cover is produced using Adobe InDesign or equivalent industry-standard design software. This approach ensures your book cover will comply with printers' specifications (including bleed allowance and trim size dimensions).

Entrusting the cover design process to a professional who has knowledge of the publishing industry will pay off many times over for you, as your final book will be indistinguishable from traditionally published books. Beyond bringing your idea to life, a professional designer has knowledge about people's perceptions of typefaces and colours and how your book cover can tap into and influence these reactions. In this way, by commissioning a professional designer to create your book's cover, you are not just paying for the final artwork; you are also receiving vital marketing advice that will be 'gold' when your published book is available for sale.

First up, you should have a clear vision of the look and feel you'd like for your book's cover prior to consulting a professional designer. The design process will be much more expensive if you have no idea what aesthetic you want at the outset. Spend time brainstorming different options for your book cover ... but try not to get carried away with your imagination and go overboard. Conversely, don't allow budget to be your sole motivator and limit what is possible. Aim to strike a balance between these two competing elements. While you'll need to be willing to spend some money to achieve a high-quality outcome for your book cover, your quest for quality doesn't have to break the bank.

Having recognised the benefits of working with a professional designer, the next challenge is to find someone who is a good fit for your budget and creative style. I'm reluctant to say this, but commissioning a professional designer can be an expensive process, particularly if you're not sure exactly what you want for your book cover. Don't rush in and simply opt for a well-known designer. Instead, you should do some initial groundwork research to find a professional designer who understands your vision for your book.

Online freelancing sites such as 99Designs and Upwork can be a good place to start your search. They offer a range of book design freelancers who can create a book cover that will tick all your boxes for a relatively modest sum. If you want a more sophisticated, upmarket cover for your book, there are also very experienced book design professionals who produce exceptional work at a more expensive price point. Remember, as an indie author, you have complete control over your book's look and feel so you can always change the cover whenever you want to later on. Therefore, if your funds are limited, consider starting off with a fairly simple cover for your book and then upgrading the original design to a more sophisticated or elaborate version down the track.

> Discuss your ideas for your book cover with several design professionals, listen to their feedback and compare their project proposals in detail. Next, check out their skill level and design portfolio. Also, consider their fees and read any reviews from previous clients. At this point, you will probably intuitively have an idea of who is the best fit for your project in terms of overall design quality, budget and delivery timelines.

Designers aren't mind-readers: developing an effective design brief

While you might assume your designer can simply 'whip out their magic wand' and produce cover artwork that's so superb your book will immediately fly off the shelf and into readers' hands, the reality is that your desires cannot be acted on if you don't voice them. This is where a design brief is invaluable.

The objective of a brief for any design project is clarity. It should provide clear expectations about the scope of the project for both the client (you) and the designer. A good design brief needs to begin with mutual understanding and the establishment of open lines of communication between both parties. This ensures that everyone is on the same page about the expected project milestones and deliverables. By communicating your expectations succinctly in the form of a design brief, your designer will be able to accurately interpret your vision to create the book cover of your dreams!

So how can you develop an effective design brief? Find a sheet of blank paper and start brainstorming any initial ideas or visual impressions you have for your book's cover. Remember, your book is likely to have a portrait orientation, while many photographs are landscape-orientated. This means that an image you think could be perfect for your cover design may not work well once it is positioned within the correct trim size dimensions for your book. Likewise, don't forget that the front cover will display as a thumbnail image on online book retail sites, so you will need to use an image that is recognisable in a smaller-sized format. If you are struggling with this exercise, spend some time researching book covers on Amazon, Book Depository and other online retailers, as well as in 'bricks and mortar' bookshops. Next, jot down what you like about those covers and try to imagine how these example front covers could form the basis of a briefing document for your designer to work with.

Having considered these basic parameters, you need to be able to articulate the specific look and feel you want for your book's cover. Do you want to use an original illustration, a single photograph or Photoshopped artwork in which several images have been merged to create a unique scene? Are you planning to write a fiction or non-fiction series, which would then mean that this initial cover will need to tie in with other book covers in the future? Documenting all this information for your designer will help them to 'get inside your head' so they can create the book cover you envision. Share your preferences regarding colours, typography, layout style, imagery, and so on with your designer, but don't make them too specific as you may curtail their creative input. Your project brief needs to clearly articulate the direction you want to head in but not constrain your designer or overload them with too many irrelevant details. The more information you provide at the outset of the project (while also remaining open to professional opinion and advice), the more likely your designer will be to achieve exactly what you have in mind for your book's cover.

It is also important to have realistic expectations about the timeline for your cover design project. You may be in a rush to get your book out to the market by a specific date, but steer clear of the 'fire brigade' approach. Leaving your design project until the very last minute when everything is in flames and only a miracle can save the situation is stressful for everyone involved. Not only do you risk compromising the quality of your book cover, you also make it difficult for your designer to deliver their best work. Creative inspiration takes time to flourish. Also, allow sufficient time for the inevitable 'back-and-forth' between you and your designer so revisions can be made to the draft cover design. Spacing out the project milestones will ensure you'll receive the ideal cover design for your book.

* * *

So having discussed the creative stages associated with preparing your manuscript for publication, we'll move on to consider the administrative aspects of publishing in chapter 9. While these steps may seem more mundane, they're just as crucial for you as an indie author, especially if your goal is to sell your book rather than simply give copies to your family and friends.

NINE

Book publishing admin: mundane but important!

If you want your published book to be available for sale to the general public, then you're probably already aware of ISBNs. Possibly you've looked at the back of a printed book, seen a series of 13 numbers listed on a barcode, and wondered what they have to do with the actual content of the book. For the reader, this barcode probably seems like just another random publication detail; however, as the author, these numbers are significant for you.

In this chapter, we'll consider the administrative aspects of publishing a book in relation to Australian authors, including the importance of ISBNs, as well as what is involved in the legal deposit process.

What is an ISBN and why do you need it for your book?

First up, ISBN is an acronym for 'international standard book number'. It is a globally recognised 13-digit marker within the publishing industry that identifies a specific book title. An ISBN provides a record of a book's metadata (including the publisher, the title and the country it was published in) and is unique to that book. ISBNs are used by publishers, booksellers, libraries and online book retailers for ordering, listing, sales records and stock control purposes. There are millions of books available for sale, so it is easier to identify a specific book by its ISBN rather than by title or author name. By purchasing an ISBN or a bulk block of 10 ISBNs (or more), you are then recorded as being the official publisher of your book. ISBNs are sold by national agencies within each country. In the USA, Bowker deals with ISBN sales, and in the UK, it is Nielsen. In Australia, the organisation responsible for issuing ISBNs is Thorpe-Bowker, and you can purchase either a single ISBN or a bulk order of 10 ISBNs directly from their website.

The numbers that make up an ISBN are grouped into five different sections. The first three numbers are known as the 'prefix element', and they are either 978 or 979. The next (single-digit) number is the 'registration group element', which indicates the book's country or language group. The third aspect is the 'registrant element', which is used to identify the publisher. Following on is the 'publication element', which identifies the format or edition of the book title. And finally, the 'check digit' is used to validate all the associated elements in the ISBN. Below is my ISBN barcode so you can see this concept 'in action'.

> Each version of a published book title (e.g. paperback, hardcover, ebook or audiobook) requires a separate ISBN. For this reason, every time you want to publish a new format of your book, you will need to use a new ISBN since they cannot be reassigned or transferred. Likewise, if you translate an existing book into a new language, it requires a new ISBN. A change to the book title, as well as any major revisions or updates to the internal content, are other reasons your book would need a new ISBN. So you can see that purchasing a block of 10 ISBNs up front is a good idea.

The difference between an ISBN and a barcode

An ISBN and the barcode on the back cover are essentially the same thing: data that identifies your book. The major difference between them is how the data is presented. An ISBN is a sequence of numbers separated by spaces or hyphens, whereas a barcode is the same sequence represented as a series of vertical lines. If you look at the numbers next to the lines in the barcode, you will observe they are exactly the same digits, occurring in the same sequence, as the ISBN. However, they serve different purposes. On its own, an ISBN is readable by humans, but if you want to include those details in a publishing database, you need to convert it into a computer-generated barcode. In other words, the barcode is the machine-readable format of an ISBN.

ISBN barcodes are mostly used by distributors and retailers to keep a record of book titles they currently have in stock. By scanning the ISBN barcode, they are able to track the complete inventory information for a specific book title. Every printed version of a book available for sale requires an ISBN barcode, which is positioned in the lower right-hand corner (or sometimes the middle) of the back cover.

It's official: the legal deposit process

After you've obtained an ISBN and have registered the metadata details for your book via the National Library of Australia's Prepublication Data Service, your book title is eligible for legal deposit. This involves sending a print or electronic copy of your published book to the National Library, as well as the relevant deposit libraries in the state in which you reside.

Legal deposit ensures that every book published in Australia can be identified and accessed by as many people as possible, both now and in the future. In addition, via the legal deposit process, books and other publications are comprehensively catalogued, which is beneficial for libraries, booksellers, publishers, scholars and the general public. And for you, as an indie author, legal deposit offers an additional avenue for you to drive awareness about your book through its inclusion in the national bibliographic database, Trove.

Legal deposit is required under the *Copyright Act 1968*, and it is considered to be your contribution towards the national objective of collecting and preserving creative works that are published by Australian authors or that relate to the people of Australia. The good news is that this process is free of charge.

For printed books, you are required to post one copy of your book to each of the relevant deposit libraries within one to two months of publication. In the case of digital publications, National edeposit (NED) is an online portal for the deposit, management, storage and preservation of published electronic material within Australia.

* * *

Chapter 9 – Book publishing admin: mundane but important!

So at this point, we've discussed all of the steps associated with the prepublication stages of your book project. In part four, we'll explore the different publication formats that are available for you to launch your book out into the world.

PART FOUR

Putting Your Best Book Forward

TEN

Which format suits your book?

Choosing the right format for your book is similar to deciding on the right outfit to wear for a special occasion. You need to pay close attention to the impression you are aiming to create. It's not just about how your outfit makes you feel (even though this is what most fashion experts will tell you!). When you are deciding what to wear for an event, you should ensure that your outfit will match the style and ambience of the occasion. So, if you are invited to a formal black-tie dinner party and you show up wearing an ensemble that is better suited to a casual brunch, you are automatically communicating a subtle message to the host that you aren't willing to respect their wishes and expectations. In a similar way, the format of your book has an impact on your readers' final opinion about its content as well as influencing who is likely to buy a copy of it.

> It is important to spend some time considering the best type of format for your published book. Remember, a range of format options are available, so you are not restricted to publishing your book in one format only.

Once you've completed all the necessary prepublication steps for your manuscript, you may decide to publish your book in as many formats as possible. By doing so, your book will be accessible to more readers, which is what most authors strive for. If your book is only available as a printed book in 'bricks and mortar' bookshops, it is more difficult for people who are not close to that physical location to purchase a copy. This, in turn, means you greatly limit your potential market share. Likewise, publishing your book title exclusively in ebook or audiobook format deprives readers who enjoy the physical experience of touching paper books of the opportunity to connect with your story.

Many indie authors are keen to publish their manuscripts as printed books; however, ebooks and audiobooks are becoming increasingly popular as well. This is not just due to their ease of use and the access they provide to a global online distribution network. In the case of ebooks, they are also one of the cheapest book formats available for readers. So, it's essential for you to factor all of these considerations into your decision-making process before you settle on which format(s) you will use to release your published book.

Common book formats for indie authors

There are three main book formats for self-publishing your manuscript. But before you make your final decision regarding your book, let's consider the pros and cons of each format.

Print books

Print books are a good option for most book genres and styles. However, it's important to be aware that this is the most expensive format for publishing your book, which will have a corresponding impact on the recommended retail price (RRP)

Chapter 10 - Which format suits your book?

you charge for it. Typically, the RRP is commensurate with the costs involved in publishing your book.

One important point if you do decide to publish printed books is to have a good distribution network in place. This involves ensuring your book is available on as many online 'print on demand' platforms as possible, including Amazon's Kindle Direct Publishing (KDP Print) and IngramSpark. The main disadvantage of printed books is the associated challenge of reaching readers who are further afield, which is why establishing a global distribution network is so important. Remember, the wider your distribution network is, the wider your marketing/sales outreach for your book will be.

Ebooks

An ebook is an electronic book that can be read on devices such as smartphones, tablets, computers or ebook readers. Unlike printed books, ebooks can be obtained by downloading them from the internet – anywhere and at anytime. Also, they are usually much cheaper to buy than print books, and they're a logical option when you are travelling as they save space and weigh nothing. Furthermore, given that many people are very attached to their smartphones, having a book that can be easily read on this platform can increase your readership base significantly. Another major advantage of ebooks is they can contain clickable links, which makes navigating between different segments of your content a breeze for readers.

Audiobooks

Audiobooks are a great option for authors whose readership base includes busy people with little (or no) time to sit down and read a print book or ebook. They allow people to do something else (such as driving or exercising) while reading. Furthermore, audiobooks are the perfect choice for people with visual impairments or those with motor control issues who struggle to hold a physical book.

Audiobooks are typically more expensive to purchase than ebooks and involve an additional production cost on your part to publish. Nevertheless, they are a very convenient lifestyle choice for many readers, so they are a good format option for you to consider.

Print is not dead! Book printing options explained

I love the digital age! At the press of a button, I can order food, arrange for tradies to fix any issues in my home and generally make my life so much easier. But when it comes to books, I am not so interested in pushing buttons. I'd much prefer to flip through the actual physical pages of a printed book. I want to be able to inhale the scent of printed paper, and I love feeling the texture of the pages of a book as I read it. And, apparently, I'm not the only person who feels this way.

According to market research undertaken by the Association of American Publishers, publishers in the USA alone made US$15.4 billion from printed book sales in 2021.[4] This was an increase of approximately 12% from sales in 2020 as the book publishing industry continued to recover from the COVID-19 pandemic. NPD Bookscan (which records approximately 85% of all worldwide print book sales) reported that sales of printed books rose by approximately 9% in 2021, with over 825 million units sold.[5]

---

4. https://www.booksandpublishing.com.au/articles/2022/01/27/209105/us-publishing-sales-up-12-aap/
5. https://www.publishersweekly.com/pw/by-topic/industry-news/financial-reporting/article/88225-print-book-sales-rose-8-9-in-2021.html

This data indicates that people are still very keen on purchasing and reading printed books. All the 'bells and whistles' associated with ebooks and audiobooks are fantastic. But at the end of the day, many of us would prefer to relax by quietly flipping through the pages of a book as we immerse ourselves in the author's imagined world.

Furthermore, in her book *How Words Get Good: The Story of the Making of a Book*, Rebecca Lee refers to studies which highlight that, due to the three-dimensional mass of printed books, it is easier to comprehend and remember words we read on paper rather than on a screen device. This is because memories are visuospatial and so are influenced by our depth perception and the composition of a physical object.

So, while you may hear much hype about ebooks and how they can be more convenient for readers, this does not mean you should immediately dismiss the print book market. Pay attention to where your potential readers are and decide on the best format for your book according to what you think will most suit their lifestyle.

Next, let's get down to the nitty-gritty of printed books and the three main types of printing formats.

Print on demand (POD)

As the heading implies, this process involves printing books in response to customer demand. In this way, when a customer purchases a book, a single copy is printed and delivered directly to them. POD can be a cost-effective option for indie authors who have budget constraints, because it eliminates having to store and handle inventory associated with printing books in bulk.

Indie authors can choose between several POD suppliers, including Amazon KDP Print, IngramSpark, Blurb and BookBaby. These services can print copies of your book *and* take care of the packaging and shipping. Most POD providers can print either black-and-white or full-colour copies of your book, and some also offer the option of printing hardback (casebound) books, as well as paperback books.

Although POD services have many advantages, there are some downsides too. In terms of per-unit printing cost, POD is the most expensive way to publish your book. In other words, it costs more per book to print one book at a time than to print a larger batch of books in one go. And despite the high unit-cost printing price, the output quality can vary depending on the provider you use. As a result, your printed book can end up looking of poor quality, particularly if it contains images. Finally, with some POD providers, tracking analytics data from book sales can be difficult.

Short-run digital printing

Short-run digital printing is a quick and cost-effective way to print smaller quantities of high-quality books. The volume of books printed using this approach is usually less than 1,000, but you can print larger quantities if you want to. The advantage of digital printing is that it is possible to publish a high-quality book without committing to a large-scale print run.

Depending on how many printed books you order at the same time, short-run digital printing is usually slightly cheaper per unit than POD services. Short-run digital printing also offers more design options in terms of cover finishes (i.e. gloss or matt celloglaze) and a wider range of higher-quality paper stock than POD. This, in turn, gives you greater control over the final look and feel of your printed book. This flexibility means that short-run digital printing is often a better option than POD if your book contains a lot of photographs or other graphics you want to showcase to best advantage.

The downside of short-run digital printing is that you are responsible for selling and shipping your books, which means that you have to store and manage inventory. So if you end up struggling to sell your book stock, short-run digital printing might actually turn out to have been a more expensive option for you. On the flipside, it can offer more diverse marketing opportunities than POD services, because you have a stock of high-quality copies of your book on hand that you can sell directly to readers at author events, seminars and conferences. You can also send free copies of your book to reviewers, which isn't practical with POD services.

Offset printing

This is the traditional method of printing books, in which text and images are transferred from a printing plate to a roller surface through a lithographic process. If you want a high-quality product for your book as well as a high-volume output (and you can afford it), then offset printing offers a premium product. It's the method used by traditional publishing companies, allowing them to sell thousands of copies of books across several print runs.

However, offset printing may not be a realistic option for indie authors. This method incurs a high initial price, because there are preliminary costs associated with setting up the printing machines and etching printing plates for your book's text and images. Offset printing also takes longer than other methods, and your books can be delayed even further if the printing company experiences paper stock or ink supply problems.

For this reason, authors usually need to order a print run of more than 1,000 books to ensure the costs associated with offset printing are financially viable. As with short-run digital printing, you are solely responsible for selling and distributing your book to your readers. This means that you'll need to find somewhere to store hundreds of copies of your published book – which, in turn, creates another expense. But if you're confident that you can sell a large number of copies, then offset printing might be the best option for your book (particularly if it's printed offshore).

So as you can see, several printing options are available for indie authors. But, as I mentioned earlier, printing books can be very expensive. The cost of a printed book is dependent on the number of pages, the type of paper stock (i.e. coated/uncoated) and the ink specifications, as well as whether you want to print it in black and white or full colour. When deciding on the print specifications for your book, you need to consider its purpose. For instance, most coffee-table books are printed on high-quality coated paper stock and have a hardcover case binding. Their internal pages are glossy with high-resolution photographic images printed in vivid colour. The printing cost for this type of book is much higher than for a paperback novel that has been printed in black and white on uncoated paper stock.

A cheap and cheerful guide to ebooks

Ebooks are a very popular format for indie authors as they are convenient, inexpensive to purchase and have a large readership base. In addition to text and images, they can contain hyperlinks and even multimedia content such as videos and audio recordings. An advantage of ebooks is that they are not restricted by location in any way, so publishing your book in ebook format will give you access to a much wider online distribution network. This means you can reach a global reading audience without having to spend the amount of money required to publish and distribute printed copies of your book.

EPUB (which stands for 'electronic publication') is the standard document file format for ebooks. Ebooks are more

Chapter 10 – Which format suits your book?

similar to websites than printed books, because the underlying structure of an EPUB is based on HTML and CSS coding. An ebook can be read on EPUB-compatible devices, including tablets, laptops, desktop computers, smartphones and specialist ereader devices. As an indie author, you can upload an EPUB version of your book for sale onto Amazon KDP and/or other online book retail sites such as Apple Books, Barnes & Noble Nook, Google Play and Kobo. Alternatively, you can use an ebook aggregator service such as Draft2Digital, Smashwords and Publish Drive to distribute your ebook so it's widely available for online sales.

Now that we've noted the advantages of ebooks as a publication format for your book, we'll discuss the two different types of ebook formats: reflowable text and fixed layout.

Reflowable text format ebooks

This is the recommended format for text-only ebooks, such as novels or memoirs, that do not have complicated page layout designs. This ebook format adapts the way the book appears on the reader's screen based on their own personal settings, including font size and style, the size of the device screen and so on.

With increasing numbers of people reading ebooks on smartphones and tablets, using a reflowable text format will ensure your ebook appeals to the largest possible audience. Readers can adjust the font size or style to suit their needs, which provides a more accessible and enjoyable reading experience. Reflowable text ebooks also have smaller file sizes, which means they take up less space on a reader's device. Also, as this format is simpler (therefore, cheaper) to create, you can sell your ebook at a more affordable retail price.

However, if your ebook contains a lot of graphics, a reflowable format can make it difficult for readers to see the images clearly. Likewise, this format can be problematic in terms of the organisation of your ebook's content, particularly if specific text needs to be positioned alongside certain images.

Fixed layout format ebooks

Fixed layout ebooks are the opposite of reflowable format ebooks. As the name implies, the content of the page is fixed, regardless of the user's setting on their phone, computer or ereader device. A fixed layout format is more suitable for books that have a strong focus on design and content structure, such as children's picture books, graphic novels or cookbooks.

Using a fixed layout format for your ebook gives you complete control over how the content is organised for readers. In this way, you can decide exactly where the text will appear in relation to any images within the ebook. Using formatting options like multiple columns or tables will also ensure that all your book's content will appear in a predetermined position within the EPUB file.

The downside of fixed layout ebooks is that they are more expensive to produce than reflowable text ebooks; you may even need to commission a specialist designer with coding expertise to undertake this task. Fixed layout ebooks produce larger-sized EPUB files, especially if the book contains lots of images, which makes them more expensive for readers to buy while also taking up more space on their device. A fixed layout format can work well if the reader uses a tablet, laptop or desktop computer, but they aren't very compatible with smartphones.

Audiobooks: a convenient product for our busy lives

An audiobook is a recording of your book being read aloud. For many older readers, this might sound like a travesty; however, times are rapidly changing, with the world becoming more complex and fast-paced. As a result, people are increasingly busy, with lots of calls on their time, so many prefer to read 'on the run' via an audiobook that they can listen to in the car or while walking the dog.

The popularity of audiobooks is growing rapidly. According to industry data from Edison Research, over 130 million people in the USA listened to an audiobook in 2021.[6] Likewise, AAP also noted that digital audiobooks continued to rise in popularity in 2021, with sales totalling nearly US$660 million and making up nearly 11% of all adult book sales.[7] The audiobook industry as a whole generated US$1.3 billion in total revenue in 2021.[8] So there's never been a better time to publish your own audiobook.

Producing an audiobook version of your book can capture a market of potential readers you might have otherwise missed. People are looking for a much more convenient way to consume information or enjoy a story, so if you make your book available in this format, you'll be able to satisfy that desire. By releasing your published book as an audiobook, you can carve out a space for yourself within the contemporary book marketplace and potentially stay ahead of your competition.

Producing an audiobook version of your book

Typically, there are two options when creating your audiobook: narrate your book yourself or hire an audiobook professional

---

6. https://www.edisonresearch.com/the-spoken-word-audio-report-2021-from-npr-and-edison-research/
7. https://www.booksandpublishing.com.au/articles/2022/01/27/209105/us-publishing-sales-up-12-aap/
8. https://www.business2community.com/digital-marketing/numbers-and-facts-you-need-to-know-about-audio-content-in-2021-02398919

to do the recording and editing for you. Narrating your book yourself is an excellent tactic if you have a nice speaking voice and the necessary recording equipment. If not, you could hire a local studio in which to record your audiobook, which gives you access to professional equipment without having to buy the gear yourself. Alternatively, hiring an audiobook professional to record and edit your book might be a more feasible option if this is something you've never done before. Obviously, it is more expensive to produce your audiobook this way; however, it may be worth it in the long run because the end result will be a high-quality product. Once the narration, recording and editing processes for your audiobook have been completed, the next step is to distribute your book to audiobook platforms for readers to purchase it.

The major players in the audiobook retail space include Audible (owned by Amazon), Apple iTunes and Google Play. Findaway Voices and Amazon's Audiobook Creation Exchange (ACX) are two popular audiobook production/distribution platforms (although ACX is not available to Australian authors). For a fee, these companies will assign you a professional narrator and then undertake the editing and post-production stages for your audiobook. They can also help you to self-publish your audiobook by distributing your title to online audiobook retailers while retaining a percentage of your sales royalties.

Alternatively, there are local audiobook production companies that can assist you with all the associated publication steps, including uploading your recording and cover image files to one of the major audiobook platforms that, in turn, will distribute your title to online retailers.

It's a good idea to spend time doing some initial research to find out which option offers you the best outcome for your audiobook.

Chapter 10 – Which format suits your book?

* * *

At this point, we've considered a range of different formats that are available for you to present your written content to readers. In part five, we'll investigate the important (and often daunting) final step – how to market and sell your book.

PART FIVE

Let's Make A Sale

ELEVEN

Book marketing for novices

Congratulations – after all your hard work, you've reached the finish line of your self-publishing journey! You can sit back, celebrate your achievement and bask in the glory of becoming a published author. Now it's time to launch your book into the world. But what do you do after the launch party is over and you've gifted printed copies of your book to family and friends? How do you create excitement and 'buzz' about your book that will entice other people to buy it?

At this point, you may be wondering why you even need to market your book. Aren't great books simply recognised on sight? Well ... no. While there are always exceptions to the rule, a book needs to be marketed if it's going to end up in the hands of readers. Unfortunately, many talented writers devote a huge amount of effort to lovingly crafting their manuscript and publishing their book but then don't bother to market it. Many authors seem to believe that if their book is available for sale on Amazon, Book Depository, Barnes & Noble or other online retail platforms, then awareness of it will somehow subliminally transplant itself into the minds of book buyers everywhere. Of course, this doesn't occur, and it's the reason why developing an effective marketing strategy is key. A well-planned marketing campaign will help you to engage readers with your story and let the quality of your writing speak for itself, inspiring them to purchase your book and also tell their friends and family.

Regardless of whether you have signed a contract with a traditional publishing company or you've opted for the self-publishing route, you'll need to do something to market your book so people become aware of it. And if you're thinking you should wait until your book is published before getting underway with marketing it, that's not so. To ensure your book receives a rousing welcome when you launch it, you should begin marketing early on in its lifecycle.

In this chapter, I'll discuss the importance of developing an effective marketing strategy and explore a few different options available to help you spread the word about your book.

> First, let's do a quick preliminary audit. By checking you've ticked all the necessary publication boxes, you will ensure your final book is of high quality so it delights the readers you're striving to reach:
>
> - *Has your manuscript been professionally edited and proofread, so your text is polished and the final book is a reasonable length? (Bloated books riddled with errors don't sell well, regardless of their theme.)*
> - *Have you paid close attention to your book's cover design, substantiating your personal preferences with background research and professional advice? (Unless you are a professional graphic designer, don't try to create the cover yourself.)*
> - *Do you have a compelling blurb with hooks that will entice readers? (You need to reel them in once they've noticed your book.)*

> - *Have you sorted out all the admin aspects (such as purchasing your ISBNs/barcode) and considered any publishing legalities for your book? (You don't want to have to deal with a problem later, once your book is available for sale.)*

DIY or outsourcing: which approach should you take?

Marketing and sales are a key aspect of the book publishing process that authors often shy away from. This is due to the misguided belief that marketing and selling books is boring and just about numbers on a spreadsheet. But this couldn't be further from the truth. Marketing simply involves making people aware of your product and then convincing them to reach into their wallets to buy it. As an author, the marketing process was kickstarted when you initially considered the internal page and cover design aesthetics of your book, as well as the blurb. However, having now reached the 'pointy end' of your publishing journey, you will need to adopt a more direct approach (and one that plays to your creative and personality strengths) to market your book and maximise its sales.

At this stage, you may be wondering if you should hire marketing or public relations experts to make this process easier and more straightforward. While this may seem like a quick-fix for book sales, the truth is that this is one area where working with professionals doesn't always guarantee success and could turn out to be an unnecessary expense. Marketing books is a relatively niche area, and many public relations and marketing companies are not familiar with its specialist publishing terminology and knowledge (including such topics as

Amazon keyword trends and book promotional platforms like BookBub).

But even if you do decide to commission a marketing professional's services, you shouldn't just sit back and hope they will make all your dreams come true. Nobody knows your book as well as you do, and nobody is as invested in getting it into readers' hands as you are. So before you head down this track, I suggest you spend some time educating yourself about book marketing. This will help you to feel more empowered and achieve better results with promoting your book to readers.

To successfully market your book, you need to be tenacious, creative and committed. Be prepared to work hard to continually publicise it to readers. After all, if you want people to read your book, you first have to be willing to tell them you've written it. Even before your book is launched into the world, you need to be constantly striving to earn readers' attention. Provide glimpses into what you're working on via social media or blog articles to build excitement about your soon-to-published book. By building trust and awareness around you as an author, you'll be in a better position to market your book once it has been published.

These days, attempting to optimally position your book in a 'bricks and mortar' bookshop isn't the primary factor in ensuring its sales success – name recognition is. For this reason, although there can be some advantages to using a pseudonym (as discussed in chapter 1), it's usually much simpler and a lot less work to market your book under your own name.

Connecting with your ideal readers

Most books only appeal to a specialised demographic. For this reason, you should try to find out more about what influences readers' decision-making processes before you begin marketing your book. As David Gaughran points out in his book, *Let's Get Digital: How to Self-Publish and Why You Should*, this is particularly the case with fiction genres. For example, readers of romance books (which, incidentally, have the largest global reading audience) don't usually purchase horror books ... and vice versa. Avoid trying to market your book to a very broad group of people, hoping to attract a few individuals who might be interested in buying it. Instead, by developing a well-defined marketing strategy, you will reach those people who are interested in your subject area or enjoy reading books within your particular genre.

Below are a few suggestions to help you find and connect with your ideal readers.

1. Consider the defining characteristics of your potential readers

While some people are spontaneous about their book purchases, many readers are very deliberate about selecting a book. The factors that can influence those choices include their age, their lifestyle, their level of education, their geographic location ... and so on. The more insight you have about the type of people who might enjoy reading your book, the more effective your marketing strategy will be and, in turn, the more likely you'll be to connect with your ideal readers.

For instance, let's imagine that you have written a book about healthy eating and weight loss. In this case, your target reading audience is people who are struggling to stay motivated to lose weight. They are probably well aware they're overweight, and they might also have some associated health challenges. Therefore, they'll be looking for books that will guide them on their weight loss journey. Even though your book might also discuss healthy lifestyles in general, it makes good sense to focus your marketing efforts on the potential audience of people who are trying to lose weight.

2. Picture your potential readers as real people

The people who will buy your book are not phantom figures somewhere out there in cyberspace. They are real people with real-life concerns and worries. Keep in mind that your book can offer them a reprieve from their daily routine or a solution to a problem they might currently be facing. Creating a marketing message that real people can connect with will ensure they'll be more likely to accept what you have to offer and, in turn, buy your book.

Make sure you incorporate a 'call to action' message in all your marketing communication so that readers are aware of what their next step should be. Your call to action could be for them to visit your website, attend your book launch or simply go to Amazon or a local bookshop and buy a copy of your book. Always ensure that your marketing message is clear, articulate and engaging.

3. Develop an awareness of what readers are searching for

Obviously, you aren't a mind-reader, so you won't know exactly what readers want. But fortunately, online platforms have an intuitive method of tracking the type of information that people (including book buyers) are searching for, which you can use to your advantage. Educate yourself about readers' search preferences by researching other books within your genre or subject area. This will help you to determine what keywords people are using to find books similar to yours. These days, most people shop for books online, so pay close attention to the SEO (search engine optimisation) data as it can have a direct influence on your book's sales success. Ensure the metadata and keywords for your book and author profiles are optimised. By using relevant words and phrases in your title, subtitle, blurb and keywords fields, you will greatly increase the visibility of your book on search engine sites such as Google, Bing and Amazon.

Having spent some time reflecting on your ideal readers and what they're looking for, let's now move on to the actual marketing process for your book.

Developing an effective marketing strategy for your book

Creating a marketing strategy for your book will increase the likelihood of it reaching a wider audience, which, in turn, will pave the way for you to become well-known as an author. And the more people who are aware of you, the greater the chance they will buy your book. Every day, people are bombarded with information telling them to buy something. With so many options available, the best method to achieve a good sales outcome for your book is to maximise its visibility so that as many people become aware of it as possible … and developing an effective marketing strategy will help you do that.

The first step is to clearly define your marketing goals. What exactly do you hope to accomplish? What does 'success' mean for you? Are you focused solely on driving sales of this one book, or are you also trying to build your profile as a writer? By clearly defining your objectives and setting a timeline for achieving them, you will be able to break them down into actionable steps to arrive at a successful outcome.

Next, you need to figure out what makes your book appealing to your ideal readers so that you can highlight those features in your marketing messages. Don't just listen to your family and friends, as they will probably say only nice things about your book because they're close to you and so can't offer an objective perspective. Instead, try to analyse your book as if you were an investigative journalist trying to work out its unique selling point and why readers might care about it.

In his book, *The Ultimate Guide to Book Marketing: The 80/20 System for Selling More Books*, Nicholas Erik refers to the '80/20 rule' (also known as the Pareto Principle) and its relevance to authors for marketing their book. He suggests that the best method of marketing your book is to develop a strategy based around your existing skills and resources. Identify and leverage as many of your natural strengths (such as being a talented creative writer, a social media wunderkind etc) as you can. This will boost your confidence about your author 'brand persona', which, in turn, can give you a competitive advantage. What may seem obvious to you is not necessarily obvious to everyone else, so identifying your own 'superpowers' is a vital step in marketing your book.

Book marketing ideas for indie authors

With the publication date for your book fast approaching, no doubt you're keen to find out what avenues are available for you to market your book. In this section we'll examine the pros and cons of each to help you decide which option(s) might best suit your specific needs.

Investigate a range of potential marketing platforms (both online and offline), as each one has something unique to offer. It's up to you to determine which platform you think would have the most traction with your ideal readers. If a lot of your readers hang out on a specific platform, obviously it makes sense to try to connect with them by focusing your energies there.

Another factor to consider is the type of marketing resources (including advertising costs etc) available on these platforms and how they might be useful for publicising your book. At this stage, I suggest you check out John Kremer's classic book, *1001 Ways to Market Your Book*, which contains a wealth of marketing ideas for indie authors.

Author platform website or blog

Having your own website or blog is a great tool for marketing your book as it increases the book's potential visibility and search capability. But remember, consumers and book buyers have become very exacting, so a basic online presence is not adequate these days. Your author website should be professionally designed, user-friendly and optimised for all platforms and devices. A well-designed online profile, combined with hard work on your part to connect with readers, will pay dividends for you in terms of book sales.

An author website or blog provides a great opportunity for you to share details about yourself *and* your book with potential readers. By posting articles about your book's subject matter/themes and sharing tips from your writing journey, you will gain organic traffic to your website, which, in turn, means that your book is more likely to appear in online searches. Communicate information you think will engage, educate and entertain your readers. Also, never miss an opportunity to make a sale by including links to any retail platforms where readers can purchase a copy of your book.

Pros

- You can set up your author platform site long before your book is published and ready to launch, to build your audience and drive engagement.
- There are no restrictions on the kind of content you can post on your own website.

- You have complete control of your website or blog (unlike social media sites, which aren't under your direct control).

Cons

- It can take a while to build an audience, particularly if you are a first-time author.
- You need to spend time regularly posting content on your platform in order to boost its SEO rankings. And that means regularly *creating* content, too.

Social media

Social media is more than just a distribution channel for your content; it's a tool for having online conversations with others via platforms such as Facebook, Twitter, Pinterest, LinkedIn and Instagram (and, increasingly, TikTok). There are even specialised book-based platforms such as Goodreads, Bookcrossing and LibraryThing, as well. Social media offers a great opportunity for you to promote yourself as a published author and communicate with readers in real time. People love to connect with the author of a book they've enjoyed reading. Publishing a book is a conduit that will allow your potential audience to 'discover' you as a writer and then become familiar with your ideas, opinions or creative passions.

Regularly post updates, upload content or share media on your social media pages to engage your readers and spark a conversation. For example, you could extract short snippets from your book and then elaborate on them to get people talking about your story or ideas. Another effective way to raise awareness about your book is to ask readers to share a picture of themselves holding a printed copy and then tagging you in their post. This helps to build a small community of devoted readers who often then evolve into becoming your superfans.

These people are usually happy to reach out to their own social networks and encourage them to become fans of your book as well.

Pros

- With the right tools, it is relatively easy to set up and manage an author page on a social media platform.
- You can connect with an interested audience straight-away, which can be very rewarding (and potentially lucrative).
- If your objective is to build relationships with potential readers and drive conversations around your book, social media is designed to do just that.

Cons

- Without an effective social media plan, you can easily get 'burned' if you make a wrong move as any fallout from a single mistake can be amplified due to the large number of people on the site.
- Unlike your own website or blog, you do not have absolute control over the content people share about you or your book.

Email marketing/newsletters

Email marketing can help you to expand your author platform so that you reach new readers, build a community of engaged fans and sell more books. Building your community, or 'tribe', via your email list and connecting with people who are already 'in your corner' allows you to more readily engage with your ideal readers. Sharing the early stages of your publishing journey with your email subscribers will help to you to stay accountable during the actual writing process so you remain on track to complete your manuscript.

If you have an established email subscriber list, you already have an audience that believes in your ideas and is ready to buy your book as soon as it is released. Then, after your book has been published, you can send out emails to launch a sale or giveaway or to communicate news related to your book business. A regular newsletter also offers an opportunity for you to ask readers for early positive reviews, which then provides you with material to leverage in your book marketing. Generally speaking, building your email subscriber list is one of the best 'return on investment' (or ROI) techniques to market your book.

Pros

- People who have subscribed to your email newsletter are more likely to buy and review your book.
- Sending email newsletters is very cost-effective, and it capitalises on your existing writing skillset!

Cons

- It can take a long time to build your email subscriber database, so it's not as useful for first-time authors.
- Email messages can end up in subscribers' spam or junk mail folders.

In-person events

As a new author, it can be very helpful to meet potential readers in person and share your story with them. In-person events, such as writers festivals, business conferences and author signing sessions in bookshops, are great opportunities for you to promote your book and build your author profile within a specific community. While this may seem daunting at first, with practice you'll becomes more comfortable with this process. These interactions will help you foster relationships that can also drive book sales. You could even offer to give a presentation at some of these events. When people identify you with a particular topic or genre, chances are they will be more open to hearing you speak about your book.

Pros
- For authors who feel confident speaking in public, this can be an excellent way to build your profile.
- It provides an opportunity for you to interact directly with prospective readers.
- It is one of the few marketing options where you can be paid while promoting your book, particularly if you are a keynote speaker at a writers festival or industry conference.

Cons
- People who are shy or suffer from stage fright may struggle to tap into this marketing option.
- Attending events can be very time-consuming and physically demanding.

Reviews and testimonials

Asking readers to post a (hopefully five-star!) review on Amazon, Google Review, Goodreads or anywhere else books are sold online is a good technique to market your book. Search engines (including Amazon) are always hunting for information that is both relevant and trustworthy. Reviews and testimonials are the social proof you need to convince more people to buy your book. On Amazon, your book's ranking (which, in turn, has a direct impact on its visibility) is influenced by the number of reviews you've received. By obtaining a large number of reviews from satisfied readers, your book will steadily climb up a search engine's rankings and your book sales will grow.

So, in addition to persuading people to buy your book, you need to figure out creative ways of encouraging them to write a review or testimonial for you. One method you can try is approaching book bloggers with a large following on social media platforms such as Facebook, Instagram or YouTube and offering to send them a free copy of your book in exchange for a review.

Pros

- It provides an opportunity for you to engage with an audience that has already enjoyed reading your book.
- If people enjoyed your book, it's likely that they will be happy to recommend it to others.

Cons

- Not everyone will love your book. Regrettably, 'haters gonna hate', which means that some people may give your book a 1- or 2-star review, regardless of its actual merit.
- It can be time-consuming to ask people to post a review for you, which means progress towards your marketing goals can be slow.

Influencer marketing

Influencers can help you get your book in front of an audience of your ideal readers, which, in turn, can drive your book's sales. Most influencers are very active on social media platforms like Facebook, Twitter, Instagram and YouTube. A 'macro-influencer' can have a large audience reach of more than a million followers, whereas 'micro-influencers' have a much smaller number of followers who are more actively engaged.

Before approaching an influencer you'd ideally like to collaborate with, it's important to do some background research about them and their areas of interest. You should ensure that your book's topic ties in with the content they typically post about. Also, spend some time figuring out who their followers are to ensure that their values and personality align with you and your book. For example, a fashion blogger is unlikely to review a book about business management or financial planning.

Pros
- The right influencer can enhance your reputation as a writer. When people see you associating with someone they consider to be credible, some of that credibility naturally rubs off on you.
- Working with an influencer can have both direct and indirect SEO benefits for your own author platform.

Cons
- Depending on the number of followers they have, working with an influencer can be very expensive.
- It can be challenging to find an influencer who will appeal to your readership base.

But wait, there's more!
As well as these marketing methods, here are some other ideas to help you spread the word about your book:
- Contact book clubs, schools, libraries and community centres and offer to give a presentation (free of charge).
- Find a local writers' group that focuses on your genre and get involved in their meetings. The conversations you'll have with established authors in the group will be invaluable for your own writing journey as well.
- Create videos (e.g. book trailers, instructional videos or vlogs) and upload them to YouTube, as they are visually engaging, more interactive and easier to consume than other types of content for some people.

Lastly, don't forget about traditional promotional avenues such as sending out a press release or writing freelance articles for local newspapers and magazines in order to get your name out in the public arena. Be willing to talk about your book and your writing journey wherever and whenever possible.

TWELVE

Positioning yourself and your book for success

You've completed all the steps involved in preparing your manuscript for publication and have developed a marketing strategy to reach potential readers. So now, it may seem as though your work is done. However, this couldn't be further from the truth. Putting your name out there to generate interest in your book and raise your profile as an author requires continuous work and effort. Granted, you have already spent considerable time (and possibly money) to ensure your book will be successful. But regardless, you still need to do what you can to build on the initial foundations you have put in place.

In this chapter, we'll explore what life after publishing your first book looks like. We will also discuss some things you can do to ensure you remain 'top of mind' as an author so your book continues to sell.

You're a published author! What's next?

Having now published your book, I'm sure you're feeling an immense sense of satisfaction for a job well done ... and you deserve to. But as I mentioned earlier, your work is not yet over.

There are still some things you need to do to capitalise on your newfound opportunities as a published author. Many authors decide to have an official book launch to celebrate this significant milestone in their lives. This is a great idea, as it creates an initial 'buzz' and excitement around introducing your book to a specific audience. However, in this chapter we'll focus on what happens *after* you've launched your book out into the world.

One thing you need to be constantly aware of is driving attention to your book to keep it fresh in readers' minds. If you 'rest on your laurels' and just wait for the sales royalties to come in, that well will dry up faster than you can imagine. Rather than hoping people will just happen to discover your book, you need to take advantage of all the promotional resources at your disposal to ensure your book remains current and top of mind.

As well as your own marketing efforts, spend some time investigating traditional media channels to promote yourself as a published author and to build awareness of your author brand. As I mentioned in the previous chapter, it can be beneficial for you to reach out to the hosts of radio shows, podcasts and even television shows. These people already have a following, so an opportunity to talk about your book in these spaces will open the door to a large pool of potential readers. Media avenues like these will give you instant credibility, which could result in you being invited as a guest speaker or panellist at a writers event (including festivals, conferences or workshops) organised around a theme relevant to your book. In these environments, you will be acknowledged as an authority figure in your field, which, in turn, increases awareness of your book and offers you more opportunities to connect with readers.

Celebrate your success

On your path to becoming a published author, you've identified your writing and publishing goals and taken steps to achieve them. Your self-publishing journey may have been riddled with roadblocks and challenges along the way, but you overcame them. By taking a moment to celebrate and acknowledge the hard work you've put in and the targets you've already achieved, you are consciously programming yourself to recognise your wins rather than focusing on how far you still have to go.

Take note of all the milestones you've accomplished so far. It's important to celebrate every success and not lose sight of your progress. Then, resolve to make a long-term plan for what your next move will be. By celebrating your victories (regardless of how small they might seem to you), you will be nurturing a success mindset that, in turn, will lead to more wins for you. Every book you sell and every good review you receive is remuneration for your hard work and dedication.

> While it's great to focus on your progress as a writer, you also need to be mindful of the importance of self-care. Having poured so much of yourself and your creative energy into the pages of your book, make sure you take some time out to recover and replenish your inner resources. In the midst of your busy life, remember to schedule moments to chill out and relax, and commit to looking after your emotional wellbeing. The expression 'take time to smell the roses' is very relevant here!

Depending on such factors as your stress levels, current workload and any sleep issues, as well as other personal problems you may be dealing with in your life, it's normal for your creativity to ebb and flow. On the other hand, creative burnout is a very real threat that you need to be on the lookout for. This level of complete physical and mental exhaustion can affect you to such an extent that it might be difficult for you to even think rationally. You can prevent creative burnout from occurring by establishing strong boundaries in your work and/or personal life. Also, ensure that you factor in regular exercise into your schedule, as well as setting aside time during the day to simply breathe and meditate. By taking care of both your physical and mental wellbeing, you will restore your balance and revive your creative spark so you can enjoy the journey to your final publishing destination.

Building on lessons learned and planning your next book

Experience is the best teacher. From the moment you first set out on your publishing journey, you need to be willing to open yourself up to the many opportunities that will emerge along the way and not take these experiences for granted. Even things that don't yield good results will, at the very least, serve as valuable lessons. Being mindful of both your successes and your failures will enhance your growth as an author and will streamline things for you when you decide to write your next book. You can never predict where inspiration will arise, so be sure to take note of any incidents on your path that might offer new creative opportunities for you. By curating your experiences and the lessons you've already learned, you are laying the foundations for your next book (or series of books).

It is much easier to market a series of books rather than a single title, so resolve to build on your first book in order to expand your readership base. If you're a fiction author, you

Chapter 12 – Positioning your book for success

could consider writing a series of novels that are linked together in some way. If you are a non-fiction author, you may decide to write multiple books on related topics that promote your expertise. By homing in on your initial writing progress, your book marketing endeavours can be more focused rather than scattering your efforts across a wide range of topics or genres.

It's important to keep in mind that change is the only constant in life. While hopefully the self-publishing advice I have shared with you in this book will stand the test of time, some of this information will undoubtedly change and evolve. We are currently living in the digital age, in which technology is progressing at a phenomenal rate. So what was relevant today could easily become obsolete tomorrow. It's those experiences you've already had in your life that will help you navigate new uncharted waters in the future.

Remember that you are about to embark on a life-changing journey that will create a personal legacy for you. This is not something that everyone gets the opportunity to do. Even though millions of books are published every year, bear in mind that every book (and the steps associated with publishing it) has its own individual story. What you are setting out to do is a wonderful testament to your creative talent and your desire to share your unique viewpoint with others. And by allocating time now to learn more about the process and develop your writing and publishing expertise, it will be easier for you whenever you're ready to take your next step on this exciting journey to authorship.

Conclusion

Now that you've reached the end of this book, it's time to reflect on the advice I have shared with you about writing and self-publishing your manuscript. As you venture forth on your self-publishing journey, no doubt you will learn many more things from your own experiences. To onlookers, writing a book may seem like a straightforward task. But they are oblivious to all the hard work that occurs behind the scenes – striving to get your creative ideas and thoughts down on the page and then transforming your written words into a polished and attractively presented published book. They often don't realise what a daunting and complicated road it can be to travel, particularly if you decide to take the self-publishing route. Throughout this book, my goal has been to be your guide and tell you about the self-publishing process without overwhelming you with information overload. I hope you'll now feel better informed and more empowered to confidently navigate your path to becoming a published author.

Whether you're working on your first book or your twentieth book, I congratulate you for having come this far. Your decision to read this book is not a random act; it indicates your genuine desire to succeed as an author. It's my sincere wish that, in the coming weeks, months or years, you'll channel this desire into action so that your dream manifests in the form of a published book. Remember, the knowledge I've shared with you is only useful when you apply it. Wisdom or information that is not acted on is impotent. You might feel anxious or fearful about what lies ahead of you, and that's quite natural. However, it's important not to allow these emotions to paralyse you. Resolve to dig deep and find the conviction within yourself to overcome your fears, face down any challenges and setbacks that will inevitably occur, and continue to move forward – one foot in front of the other.

It's wonderful that you've decided to share your knowledge or imaginative story with others. Many people talk about writing a book, but only a relatively small number actually end up doing it. Even if your book doesn't win a literary prize or become a bestseller, you still have a lot to celebrate. Simply by writing your manuscript, you are announcing to the world that you are an author. And taking the ensuing steps to self-publish your book is a signal to others that you honour your creativity and life experiences.

As you embark on your self-publishing journey, I feel privileged to have played a small part along the way. I would love to hear about your progress as a published author, because the story does not end here. As a matter of fact, I hope this book will be the catalyst for you to begin the next chapter in your writing and publishing adventure.

I'm looking forward to seeing the reward of all your hard work when your published book is available online or on bookshop shelves. Here's to your future success in the exciting world of book publishing!

Next steps

My aim in sharing my knowledge and expertise in this book has been to help you to capitalise on your writing talents so you become a published author. Armed with this information, hopefully you'll now feel better equipped to move forward and accomplish your publishing goals.

So where to from here? Self-publishing your book is a steep hill for anyone to climb by themselves. But the good news is that you don't have to walk this path alone. While some authors do attempt to DIY all the self-publishing steps for their book, doing it well usually involves a team approach. The Brisbane Self Publishing Service team and I 'live and breathe' book publishing, and we've been closely involved in the publication of more than 100 books during the past eight years. Along the way, I developed my five-step Let's Get Published Framework® to support writers like you to achieve the exciting milestone of publishing a book. So depending on where you currently are with your book, outlined below are three ways you can take action now towards achieving your publishing goals.

1. Sign up for my free online course

Not ready to take the plunge yet? You can learn more about my self-publishing framework and how it can work for your book by signing up for my free online course using the following link:

> https://www.brisbaneselfpublishing.com.au/self-publishing-email-course-sign-up/

2. Schedule an author publishing consultation

Keen to discuss your book project and how you can get underway with your self-publishing journey in more detail? If so, you might like to schedule an author publishing consultation via phone, Zoom online meeting or in person (Brisbane-based authors only) with me. During these mentoring-style sessions, you can 'pick my brain' and ask any questions you have about the steps involved in self-publishing your book. For more information about my author publishing consultations, please check out the details on the following page of the Brisbane Self Publishing Service website:

> https://www.brisbaneselfpublishing.com.au/author-publishing-consultations/

3. Contact me for a quote

Ready to get the ball rolling? If you're 'good to go' and want to get started straightaway on all the steps involved in preparing your manuscript for publication, I'd love to provide a quote for your project. Just fill in the form on my website Contact page or send me an email (kirsty@brisbaneselfpublishing.com.au) so we can embark on your book publishing journey together.

> https://www.brisbaneselfpublishing.com.au/contact/

References and resources

Notes

1. Wikipedia Encyclopedia article (last edited 3 August 2022) 'SMART criteria', https://en.wikipedia.org/wiki/SMART_criteria
2. Arts Law Centre of Australia (last reviewed 2022) 'Defamation Law', https://www.artslaw.com.au/information-sheet/defamation-law/
3. The Book Smugglers (27 April 2010) 'Cover matters: the survey results', blog post, https://www.thebooksmugglers.com/2010/04/cover-matters-the-survey-results.html
4. Books and Publishing (27 January 2022) 'US publishing sales up 12%: AAP', https://www.booksandpublishing.com.au/articles/2022/01/27/209105/us-publishing-sales-up-12-aap/
5. Milliot, Jim (6 January 2022), 'Print books had a huge sales year in 2021', *Publishers Weekly*, https://www.publishersweekly.com/pw/by-topic/industry-news/financial-reporting/article/88225-print-book-sales-rose-8-9-in-2021.html
6. Edison Research (11 November 2021), 'The spoken word audio report', blog post, https://www.edisonresearch.com/the-spoken-word-audio-report-2021-from-npr-and-edison-research/

7. Books and Publishing (27 January 2022) 'US publishing sales up 12%: AAP', https://www.booksandpublishing.com.au/articles/2022/01/27/209105/us-publishing-sales-up-12-aap/
8. Jaworski, Ron (14 July 2022), 'Numbers and facts you need to know about audio content in 2021', *Business 2 Community: Digital marketing*, https://www.business2community.com/digital-marketing/numbers-and-facts-you-need-to-know-about-audio-content-in-2021-02398919

Books

American Psychological Association (2020) *Publication manual of the American Psychological Association*, 7th edition, American Psychological Association.

Bache, Stuart (2018) *The author's guide to cover design*, Books Covered.

Erik, Nicholas (2020) *The ultimate guide to book marketing: The 80/20 system for selling more books*, Nicholas Erik.

Flann, Elizabeth, Hill, Beryl and Wang, Lan (2014) *The Australian editing handbook*, 3rd edition, John Wiley and Sons.

Friedlander, Joel (2018) *The book blueprint: Expert advice for creating industry-standard print books*, 2nd edition, Marin Bookworks.

Gaughran, David (2020) *Let's get digital: How to self-publish and why you should*, 4th edition, David Gaughran.

Kawasaki, Guy and Welch, Shawn (2015), *APE – author, publisher, entrepreneur: How to publish a book*, Nononina Press.

Kremer, John (2014) *1001 ways to market your book*, 6th edition, Open Horizons Publishing.

Lee, Rebecca (2022) *How words get good: The story of the making of a book*, Profile Books.

Martin, Tiffany Yates (2020) *Intuitive editing: A creative and practical guide to revising your writing*, FoxPrint Inc.

Oxford University Press editorial staff (2016) *New Oxford style manual*, Oxford University Press.

Penn, Joanna (2016) *The successful author mindset: A handbook for surviving the writer's journey*, Curl Up Press.

Ramsay, Margaret (2018) *The complete guide to English usage for Australian students*, 6th edition, Cengage Learning.

Strunk, William and White, EB (2000) *The elements of style*, 4th edition, Allyn & Bacon.

University of Chicago Press editorial staff (2017) *The Chicago manual of style*, 17th edition, University of Chicago Press.

Whitbread, David (2009) *The design manual*, revised and expanded edition, UNSW Press.

Useful websites

Chapters 1–3: Writing/publishing

Author Accelerator (online community of book coaches): https://www.bookcoaches.com/

The Creative Penn – Joanna Penn (writing resources and guides): https://www.thecreativepenn.com/

Evernote: https://evernote.com/

Google Docs: https://www.google.com.au/docs/about/

Jane Friedman (author advice and book industry news): https://www.janefriedman.com/

Reedsy (publishing industry freelancers, tools and resources site): https://reedsy.com/

Scrivener (software for writing and managing book manuscripts): https://www.literatureandlatte.com/

Story Grid (editing methodology and writing community): https://storygrid.com/

The Writer Finder (freelance copywriter/ghostwriter service): https://www.thewriterfinder.com/

Writers Digest (writing community, magazine and resource centre): https://www.writersdigest.com/

Upwork (global freelancing site): https://www.upwork.com/

Chapters 4–6: Editing and proofreading (including legal considerations)

Arts Law Centre of Australia (legal advice and information for writers and arts practitioners): https://www.artslaw.com.au/

Australian Copyright Council (general copyright information): https://www.copyright.org.au/

Australian Government Style Manual (guide to Australian Government text style conventions): www.stylemanual.gov.au

Australian Society of Authors (professional association for Australian authors and illustrators): https://www.asauthors.org/

Chartered Institute of Editing and Proofreading, UK (CIEP): https://www.ciep.uk/

Conscious Style Guide: https://consciousstyleguide.com

Creative Commons: https://creativecommons.org/

Disability Language Style Guide: https://ncdj.org/style-guide/

Editorial Freelancers Association, USA (EFA): https://www.the-efa.org/

Fox Print Editorial – Tiffany Yates Martin (editorial guides, resources and advice): https://foxprinteditorial.com/

GLAAD Media Reference Guide: https://www.glaad.org/reference

Grammarly (writing and editing tool): https://www.grammarly.com/

Institute of Professional Editors, Australia and New Zealand (IPEd): https://www.iped-editors.org/

Macquarie Dictionary: https://www.macquariedictionary.com.au/

People With Disability Australia (PWDA) Language Guide: https://pwd.org.au/resources/language-guide/

PerfectIt (consistency checking software): https://intelligentediting.com/

Chapters 7–8: Book design

ASA Style File (source of Australian freelance illustrators): https://asastylefile.com/

The Book Designer – Joel Friedlander (advice and articles about book design): https://www.thebookdesigner.com/

DepositPhotos (stock image library): https://depositphotos.com/

99Designs.com (source of freelance designers for book covers and other graphics): https://99designs.com.au/

Shutterstock (stock image library): https://www.shutterstock.com/

Chapter 9: Book publishing administration

National edeposit (legal deposit for Australian published electronic material): https://ned.gov.au/ned/

National Library of Australia (Prepublication Data Service and legal deposit in Australia):
https://www.nla.gov.au/using-library/services-publishers/prepublication-data-service
https://www.nla.gov.au/using-library/services-publishers/legal-deposit

Thorpe-Bowker Identifier Services (ISBN supplier in Australia): https://www.myidentifiers.com.au/

Trove (bibliographic database maintained by the National Library of Australia): https://trove.nla.gov.au/

Chapter 10: POD, ebook and audiobook distribution services

Amazon Kindle Direct Publishing (ebook and POD printing/distribution): https://kdp.amazon.com/en_US/

Blurb (POD printing and distribution): https://au.blurb.com

BookBaby (ebook and POD distribution): https://www.bookbaby.com/

Draft2Digital (ebook aggregator service): https://www.draft2digital.com/

Findaway Voices (audiobook production and aggregator service): https://www.findawayvoices.com/

IngramSpark (POD printing and distribution): https://www.ingramspark.com/

PublishDrive (ebook aggregator service): https://publishdrive.zendesk.com/hc/en-us

Smashwords (ebook aggregator service): https://www.smashwords.com/

Chapter 11: Book marketing

BookBub (book discovery service): http://www.bookbub.com

David Gaughran (newsletters, books and online courses): https://davidgaughran.com/

Goodreads (book reviewing site): https://www.goodreads.com/

Kindlepreneur – Dave Chesson (Kindle marketing strategies for authors): https://kindlepreneur.com/

LibraryThing: https://www.librarything.com/

Nicholas Erik (coaching and resources): https://nicholaserik.com/

Self Publishing Formula – Mark Dawson (podcast, online courses and other resources): https://selfpublishingformula.com/

General indie publishing information

Alliance of Independent Authors, UK (ALLi): https://www.allianceindependentauthors.org/

Independent Book Publishers Association, USA (IBPA): https://www.ibpa-online.org/

Small Press Network (represents small and independent publishers in Australia): https://smallpressnetwork.com.au/

Acknowledgements

Thank you from the bottom of my heart to my wonderful husband, David, who patiently listened to my never-ending litany of self-doubt and uncertainty while I was writing this book manuscript. Thanks for your calm strength and for always encouraging me to 'dream big and reach for the stars'.

I'm eternally grateful for my awesome family. Special thanks to my mum and dad, my beautiful children – Claire, Chris and Rachel – and my brother, Matthew. You guys rock!

To my dear friends, Debbie and Wendy – I'm blessed having both of you 'in my corner'.

A huge vote of thanks to my fabulous 'edibuddies' – Patrice Shaw, Lee Ellwood, Charlotte Cottier and Judy Fredriksen – for your wise counsel to ensure my book became a reality, as well as your ongoing help, enthusiasm and good humour with my self-publishing business adventures. How fortunate am I to be able to collaborate regularly with such a talented bunch of professional women? Go girl power!

I'm indebted to such indie publishing 'rock stars' as Michael Hanrahan and Andrew Griffiths from Australian Business Book Awards; Jim Higgins from Fellowship of Australian Writers (Qld); Russell Perry from Australian Authors Marketplace; Gillian Lloyd from Brisbane Writers

Group Convention; Gazel Kilicdogan from Pegasus Media & Logistics; Ben Aitchison and Michael McDermaid from Paradigm Print Media; Simone Feiler from Brisbane Audiobook Production; Lisa DeSpain and Erica Smith from Ebookconverting.com; Janhavi Khule (ebook conversion specialist); and Author Accelerator certified book coach Bev Ryan, for your generous support and for being guiding lights on my path. Thanks also to Mick Cullen, Alison McGrath, Dallas McMillan and Glen Carlson for your constructive advice when I was a newbie business owner, as well as to Gabby Lambkin for graciously helping me to navigate my 'second Saturn return' challenges.

Finally, to all my aspiring author clients, referral partners and the other creative and interesting people I've met since first launching Brisbane Self Publishing Service – I feel privileged that you've shared your thoughts with me and that I get to work in such a cool industry. Lucky me!

About the author

Kirsty Ogden began her career working in libraries before deciding to switch directions and study graphic design, graduating with a communication and design degree in 2007.

Following a brief stint working in marketing roles, Kirsty was keen to return to the world of books, so she undertook a postgraduate course in editing and publishing. After completing this qualification, she set up her own freelance editing and design business, Epiphany Editing & Publishing.

In 2014, Kirsty launched another business – Brisbane Self Publishing Service – to offer aspiring authors a one-stop shop to self-publish their books. Since then, she has established a trusted network of publishing professionals and supported numerous indie authors on their self-publishing journey.

Kirsty is married and has three millennial children. She lives in sunny Brisbane, where she enjoys reading well-written (as well as edited and designed!) books and sharing her love for all things publishing.

For more information about Kirsty and her self-publishing services for indie authors, check out her LinkedIn profile:

https://www.linkedin.com/in/kirstyogden/

www.ingramcontent.com/pod-product-compliance
Lightning Source LLC
Chambersburg PA
CBHW050313010526
44107CB00055B/2220